LIBRARY ANALYTICS AND METRICS

Using data to drive decisions and services

LIBRARY ANALYTICS AND METRICS

Using data to drive decisions and services

Edited by
Ben Showers

facet publishing

Published by Facet Publishing,
7 Ridgmount Street, London WC1E 7AE
www.facetpublishing.co.uk

Facet Publishing is wholly owned by CILIP: the Chartered Institute of Library
and Information Professionals.

British Library Cataloguing in Publication Data
A catalogue record for this book is available from the British Library.

ISBN 978-1-85604-965-8

First published 2015

Text printed on FSC accredited material.

Typeset from editor's files by Facet Publishing Production in 10/13 pt Palatino
Linotype and Myriad Pro.
Printed and made in Great Britain by CPI Group (UK) Ltd, Croydon, CR0 4YY.

Dedication
To Jennie, Willow and Rowan

Contents

List of figures and tables xi

Contributors xiii

Acknowledgements xxiii

Introduction: getting the measure of analytics and metrics xxv
    Library analytics...xxv
    The streetlight effect xxvi
    Learning analytics..xxvii
    About this book...xxviii
    Chapter summaries..xxviii
    Analytics and metrics: a brief note on definitions................................xxix
    References...xxx

1   Library data: big and small 1
    Chapter overview 1
    Defining big and small data 2
    Small and big data in libraries 3
    CASE STUDY 1.1 The potential of data to inform personalized
    recommendations at the Open University Library 5
    Richard Nurse
    CASE STUDY 1.2 Library 'big data': developing a shared analytics service
    for academic libraries 14
    Ben Showers
    Chapter conclusion 20
    Big and small data: further resources 21
    References 21

2   Data-driven collections management **23**
Chapter overview...23
The collections turn 24
Managing the local collection..24
Managing the 'national' collection..27
CASE STUDY 2.1 Building an analytics toolkit at the Harvard
Library 28
Kim Dulin and Carli Spina
CASE STUDY 2.2 Collection management analytics: the Copac Collection
Management tools project...35
Shirley Cousins and Diana Massam
Chapter conclusion 44
Data-driven collections management: further resources 44
References 45

3   Using data to demonstrate library impact and value **47**
Chapter overview...47
Does library use have an impact on student success? 47
Taking analytics seriously...48
The ethics of impact..50
CASE STUDY 3.1 Library impact data: investigating library use and
student attainment (University of Huddersfield) 51
Graham Stone
CASE STUDY 3.2 Retention, student success and academic engagement
at Minnesota (University of Minnesota)..58
Shane Nackerud, Jan Fransen, Kate Peterson and Kristen Mastel
CASE STUDY 3.3 The Library Cube: revealing the impact of library use on
student performance (University of Wollongong)................................66
Brian Cox and Margie Jantti
Chapter conclusion: from knowing to showing! 74
Library impact and value: further resources 75
Notes 75
References 76

**4   Going beyond the numbers: using qualitative research to
transform the library user's experience**...**79**
Chapter overview...79
Qualitative research and the user experience.....................................79
Qualitative research and emerging user needs 81
A mix of skills and methodologies...81
CASE STUDY 4.1 Utilizing qualitative research methods to measure
library effectiveness: developing an engaging library experience.....82
Lynn Silipigni Connaway, Erin M. Hood and Carrie E. Vass
CASE STUDY 4.2 Ethnographic techniques and new visions for libraries.......96
Donna Lanclos

Chapter conclusion...108
Qualitative library research: further resources.......................................108
Note 109
References...109

5 Web and social media metrics for the cultural heritage sector........113
Chapter overview 113
Web metrics and analytics in the cultural heritage sector 114
The social web 114
The future of web metrics 116
CASE STUDY 5.1 The web impact of cultural heritage institutions.............117
David Stuart
CASE STUDY 5.2 Let's Get Real: a Journey Towards Understanding
and Measuring Digital Engagement 136
Sejul Malde, Jane Finnis, Anra Kennedy, Elena Villaespesa, Seb Chan and
Mia Ridge
Chapter conclusion...150
Web and social media metrics: further resources..................................150
References...151

6 Understanding and managing the risks of analytics 153
Chapter overview 153
Redrawing the boundaries of privacy...153
Whose data is it anyway?..154
The importance of data flows 155
CASE STUDY 6.1 The legal, risk and ethical aspects of analytics..................157
Ian Chowcat, David Kay and Naomi Korn
Chapter conclusion...166
Understanding the risks of analytics: further resources.........................166
References...166

7 Conclusion: towards a data-driven future?...................................169
Reference...170

Index 171

Figures and tables

Figures

1.1   Improving the data in your recommender system 8
1.2   RISE user interface..9
1.3   A simple relevancy algorithm..10
1.4   Example of the kind of data delivered by the LAMP 'ugly prototype':
      loans activity for a specific subject, broken down by gender..................18
2.1   Initial wireframes for dashboard..32
2.2   Modified Harvard library explorer dashboard..32
2.3   'Bubble' visualization wireframe for the Harvard library explorer
      dashboard...33
2.4   CCM tools results visualization: the graphical presentation of a result
      set showing the number of documents held by each contributor
      within the search results...37
2.5   Extract from York collection profile: data exported from CCM tools
      used to generate locally tailored graphs...41
3.1   Correlation between electronic resource usage and student grades..........71
3.2   Correlation between borrowing and student grades................................72
4.1   Emerging groups and human sources...88
4.2   Emerging groups and digital sources..89
4.3   Educational stages and databases..90
4.4   Educational stages and decision..91
4.5   Educational stages and contact..91
4.6   Part of the ground floor in Atkins Library, Spring 2012 (photo by
      M. McGregor)...98
4.7   Students working at a whiteboard..99
4.8   Student on sofa while another draws on the whiteboard.......................99
4.9   Student referring to textbook while another uses the whiteboard.........100
4.10 Whiteboard and large computer screen near the sitting area (Photo
      by M. McGregor)..100
4.11 Flexible study space being used by students (Sketch by M. McGregor)...101
4.12 Touch-screen tables..102

4.13   Group study rooms 102
4.14   Café-style seating space outside the library café...............................103
4.15   Highly configurable space...103
4.16   Zoning use diagram: eating zones 104
4.17   Zoning use diagram: study zones..105
4.18   Zoning use diagram: talking zones..105
4.19   Zoning use diagram: eating and studying zones 106
4.20   Zoning use diagram: studying and talking zones 106
4.21   Zoning use diagram: studying and laptop zones 107
5.1   Web metrics tools and methodologies considered by this case study......121
5.2   'Hits' received by the UK Government Web Archive hosted by the
       National Archives (National Archives, 2012)..122
5.3   'British Museum' and 'Terracotta Army' as seen through Google Trends 124
5.4   Network diagram of URL citations between five CHIs 131
5.5   Social network of the UK's most-visited CHIs......................................134

Tables

1.1   Survey results for the value of different types of recommendations............11
3.1   Dimensions of usage 53
3.2   Demographic data examined in Phase 2 54
3.3   Discipline variables..55
3.4   Weighted average marks (WAM) for undergraduate students
       (Faculty of Business) against annual electronic resource usage
       frequency (hours)..72
4.1   Educational stages and number of participants in each stage 85
5.1   Visitor numbers and Alexa Traffic Rank for five CHIs 123
5.2   Prominent social media of the five CHIs 125
5.3   Estimated number of results for organizational names in Google.............128
5.4   The number of inlinks and linking domains for the five CHIs
       according to three different SEO sites..130
5.5   Impact of websites on social media platforms 132
5.6   Total Twitter followers and centrality of the five CHIs.......................134

Contributors

Seb Chan

Seb Chan is currently Director of Digital and Emerging Media at the Cooper-Hewitt Smithsonian National Design Museum in New York. He has been responsible for the Museum's recent digital renewal and its transformation into an interactive, playful new museum, re-opened after a three-year rebuilding and re-imagining. Prior to relocating to New York, he was Head of Digital, Social and Emerging Technologies at the Powerhouse Museum in Sydney, where he led teams responsible for the Powerhouse's pioneering work throughout the 2000s in open access, mass collaboration, web metrics and digital engagement, as well as large-scale Australian cross-agency projects.

Seb also led a parallel life in electronic art and music organizing, curating festivals and international touring, and was founding editor-in-chief of a long-running music magazine.

Ian Chowcat

Dr Ian Chowcat has over 20 years' experience in using digital technology in learning and teaching. For many years he was an Associate Lecturer for the Open University, teaching distance courses in humanities and technology, including the entirely online MA in Philosophy. In the late 1990s he helped pioneer the training of OU Arts tutors in online teaching and research. He worked as an e-learning facilitator for Ufi/learndirect and the National College for School Leadership, and from 2005 to 2008 was Director of the South Yorkshire e-Learning Programme, then the largest regional e-learning programme in the EU. Since 2008 he has been Head of Learning Innovation for Sero Consulting Ltd, working on many assignments for Becta, Jisc, and local and regional authorities, covering e-learning, digital inclusion and digital information projects, as well as project managing the establishment of both of Sheffield's University Technical Colleges. A former civil servant in the Department for Education, he has a doctorate in Philosophy. He has taught at the University of Sheffield in both the Philosophy department and the management school, and helps to facilitate a MOOC in modern and contemporary American poetry run by the University of Pennsylvania. He lives in Sheffield and is married with one daughter.

Lynn Silipigni Connaway

Dr Lynn Silipigni Connaway is a Senior Research Scientist at OCLC Research. She leads the User Behavior and Synthesis Activities at OCLC Research and is the Chair of the ALA ACRL Value of Academic Libraries Committee. Lynn held the Chair of Excellence position at the Departmento de Biblioteconomía y Documentación at the Universidad Carlos III de Madrid and collaborated with the faculty on user-centered research. She was a Visiting Researcher in the Department of Information Studies, University of Sheffield and a Visiting Scholar at the Royal School of Library and Information Science, Copenhagen, Denmark. She has received research funding from the IMLS in the USA and Jisc and the Arts and Humanities Research Council in the UK. She leads OCLC Research in the digital visitors and residents project and is the co-principal investigator of an IMLS-funded project with Rutgers University to investigate the possibility of seamless collaboration between knowledge institutions such as libraries and the Social Q&A (SQA) community. Lynn is the co-author of the fourth and fifth editions of *Basic Research Methods for Librarians* (Libraries Unlimited) and has authored numerous other publications. She is frequently an international and national speaker on the topic of how individuals get their information and engage with technology, and on the assessment and development of user-centred library services. Prior to joining OCLC Research, she was the Vice-President of Research and Library Systems at NetLibrary, the director of the Library and Information Services Department at the University of Denver, and on the faculty of the Library and Informational Science program at the University of Missouri, Columbia.

Shirley Cousins

Shirley Cousins is the Copac Service Manager, dealing with the day-to-day running of the Copac service as well as being involved with planning, managing and participating in a range of project activity, including the Copac Collection Management Tools project. Shirley has been at Mimas, the UK National Data Centre at the University of Manchester, since 1995. She has worked on the design and development of the Copac service since its inception, as well as having more recent involvement with Zetoc development activity. Her background is in information retrieval, doing research and lecturing in the Department of Information and Library Studies, University of Wales Aberystwyth.

Brian Cox

Brian Cox has worked in a wide variety of roles, including privacy, copyright, records management, quality, program management and planning. He started his professional career in privacy, where he worked in both policy and compliance for the Office of the Federal Privacy Commissioner. He then moved to the University of Wollongong (UOW), where he dramatically reduced copyright risk through a mixture of education and audits, underpinned by Copyright Policy and Guidelines. He overhauled the Library's operational data – transforming it from an unreliable, highly varied, complex and difficult to navigate structure, into highly reliable and easily accessible data. He also played a key role in transforming planning and performance reporting, where through championing project management and a much simplified but more coherent planning and reporting structure, he was able to greatly simplify the Executive's task of strategic stewardship. Brian first developed his vision for the Library Cube when he started working with quality, where with the support of the Library Executive he worked with the University's Performance Indicators Unit to transform his vision into reality. Since then, Brian has been seconded to the Peer Learning Unit at UOW, where he made great contributions to improving processes, delivering real and significant ongoing savings for that unit.

Kim Dulin

Kim Dulin serves as Associate Director for Collection Development and Digital Initiatives at the Harvard Law Library and Director of the Harvard Library Innovation Lab. She has been an academic law librarian since 1988. In addition to her experience as an academic law librarian, Kim has served as a practising attorney and an adjunct professor of law. Kim has a JD from the University of Iowa College of Law, an MS from the University of Illinois Graduate School of Library and Information Science, and a BA from the University of Iowa.

Jane Finnis

Jane Finnis is the Chief Executive of Culture24 (WeAreCulture24.org.uk). She is an experienced strategist, producer and communicator with a deep understanding of audiences, digital tactics and tools. She has worked in the arts professionally since 1989 and is often invited to write and speak about her work at conferences in the UK and around the world.

Jan Fransen

Jan Fransen is the Service Lead for Researcher and Discovery Systems for University of Minnesota Libraries in the Twin Cities. In that role, she works across Libraries divisions and with campus partners to provide library systems that save researchers' and students' time and improve their access to the materials they need to get to their next steps.

Jan's previous library experience was as an engineering liaison librarian, working with faculty and students in her alma mater, the College of Science and Engineering at the University of Minnesota. Before becoming a librarian in 2008, Jan had a career as a programmer, trainer and writer, with a focus on helping people use technology to be more effective in their jobs.

Erin M. Hood

Erin M. Hood MLIS is a Research Support Specialist at OCLC Research. She received her undergraduate degree in Religious Studies from Otterbein College and her graduate degree in Library and Information Science from Kent State University. She is currently working on the Digital Visitors and Residents study with the University of North Carolina, Charlotte, funded by Jisc. She also regularly contributes to other OCLC Research studies, including Cyber Synergy, the User Behavior Report, and WorldCat Survey Report. She previously worked on the IMLS-funded study, Seeking Synchronicity, in combination with Rutgers, The State University of New Jersey, and the Digital Information Seeker Report.

Margie Jantti

As the Director, Library Services at the University of Wollongong (UOW) Australia, Margie Jantti provides leadership and direction for library services spanning six onshore campus locations and guidance for offshore library partnerships in the UAE and Asia. She is an active member of UOW policy and governance committees. She is the Deputy President of the Council of Australian University Librarians (CAUL), and for a number of years chaired the CAUL Quality Assessment Advisory Committee. She contributes to the CAUL and Council of Australian University Directors of IT (CAUDIT) Leadership Institutes.

Key outcomes at UOW Library for the past five years include: significant restructuring of the organization to extend capacity to support the research community, the creation of the Library Cube (an enterprise reporting system focusing on the impact of library resource usage and students' academic performance), and revitalized approaches to organizational performance monitoring and reporting frameworks.

David Kay

David Kay is a UK-based consultant at Sero Consulting (www.serohe.co.uk), which he co-founded in 2004 after over 20 years working in systems design for education and library management. David began investigating the potential of activity data and analytics in connection with Higher Education libraries in the Jisc TILE project (2009). He has subsequently been involved in Jisc's ongoing examination of those concepts in the MOSAIC demonstrator project, in the synthesis of the 2011 Activity Data program (http://activitydata.org) and in the LAMP project (http://jisclamp.mimas.ac.uk/2014/01/so-what-do-we-mean-when-we-say-analytics).

He has co-authored articles in the CETIS series on analytics and the whole institution and on legal and ethical considerations (2012) and an analytics White Paper for Innovative Interfaces in 2013 (www.iii.com/sites/default/files/Innovative_Conversation_Analytics.pdf). In 2014 he presented a keynote speech at the ARL Assessment Conference on the role of the library in unravelling the cat's cradle of activity data.

Anra Kennedy

Anra Kennedy is responsible for the development and delivery of Culture24's web publishing, content strategy and partnerships. This includes editorial, research and data aggregation services for clients, including the BBC, Europeana and the Centenary Partnership. An ex-teacher, she is also a trustee of Kids in Museums and GEM (Group for Education in Museums).

Naomi Korn

Naomi Korn is an IP Consultant specializing in copyright, rights management and licensing for clients from across the UK's public sector (www.naomikorn.com). She has been running all of ASLIB's copyright training for a number of years.

Naomi is the Chair of LACA (Libraries and Archives Copyright Alliance) and a founder member of the MuseumsIP Network. She sits on the Executive Committee of the Museums Copyright Group and on the Advisory Panel of the Public Catalogue Foundation. Much of her work includes lobbying and advocacy on behalf of museums, libraries and archives.

Naomi has a prolific publishing portfolio covering an eclectic range of copyright and licensing topics, which includes multiple briefing papers, blogs, tools and templates. She also regularly writes a copyright surgery column for the *Managing Information* journal and other publications.

Donna Lanclos

Dr Donna Lanclos has been the Library Ethnographer at the J. Murrey Atkins Library at University of North Carolina (UNC) Charlotte since 2009. Her research interests include the nature of information seeking behaviour, as well as the relationship of the needs of instructors and learners to the physical and virtual spaces of academic libraries, and in higher education generally. She has done research at University College London, as well as in and around the UNC Charlotte campus. Donna's training is in folklore as well as socio-cultural anthropology, and she earned her PhD in Anthropology from the University of California, Berkeley, in 1999. Her research on the folklore of primary school children in Northern Ireland was published in 2003 by Rutgers University Press as *At Play in Belfast: Folklore and the Formations of Identity in Northern Ireland*. She has published several articles in LIS, IT, folklore and anthropology journals.

Sejul Malde

Sejul Malde is Research Manager at Culture24, and works on a range of projects, both UK and European wide, all of which at their core aim to help cultural organizations, and the wider sector, become better at understanding and engaging audiences digitally. In particular he co-leads Culture24's collaborative action research projects, Let's Get Real. He has significant experience in both the commercial and cultural sectors, and is interested in exploring opportunities for more meaningful audience engagement through cross sector learning and collaboration.

Diana Massam

Diana Massam joined Mimas, the UK National Data Centre at the University of Manchester, in 2007, as a project manager working to deliver new and existing services for libraries, researchers and end users. While contributing to the work of the Copac Collection Management Tools project, she is also currently involved in managing a project researching metadata enhancement techniques and their impact on users, and working with Arthritis Research UK developing content for their website. Before joining Mimas she was a senior library manager at Manchester Metropolitan University for several years, where she managed the delivery of information literacy services as well as a busy business library. Diana has been a member of the UKSG Education Subcommittee since 2009.

Kristen Mastel

Kristen Mastel is an outreach and instruction librarian at the University of Minnesota. She received her Master of Library Science from Indiana University, and her undergraduate Bachelor of Arts in speech communication from the University of Minnesota–Morris. Her research areas of interest include instruction, information literacy, outreach and instructional design. Kristen is Past President of the Minnesota Library Association.

Shane Nackerud

Shane Nackerud has worked at the University of Minnesota–Twin Cities for 16 years, currently as Technology Lead for the Library Initiatives. In his current position he is working on finding new ways of integrating library content and open textbooks and resources into courses and curricula, and assisting faculty and researchers publish open scholarly content using library publishing tools and services. Shane's research interests include library use assessment, libraries and e-learning, resource integration, academic publishing and web design. He received a BA in history from Augustana College in 1994 and his MLS from Indiana University in 1995.

Richard Nurse

Richard Nurse is Library Services Manager: Digital Services Development at the Open University Library Services and is responsible for managing library websites, developing funding opportunities and managing the delivery of key strategic library projects. Current projects include the development of the Open University Digital Archive to preserve and showcase material from the collections of the Open University archive, and the Library Futures project, which is carrying out research into student needs of library search, procuring and implementing a next generation library management system, and developing a Digital Skills Passport. Richard has also been involved with the LMS Change project and the Jisc Library Analytics and Metrics Project as a member of the Community Advisory and Planning Group.

Richard has been at the Open University since 2009 and previously spent more than 20 years working in public libraries managing library IT services, bibliographical services and heritage services. His research interests are in activity data, digital libraries, linked data and library technology in general.

Kate Peterson

Kate Peterson is the Undergraduate Services Librarian at the University of Minnesota–Twin Cities. She also works with Writing Studies, First Year Writing and Orientation. She has previously worked at California State University–Long Beach, St. Cloud State University and Capella University.

Mia Ridge

Dr Mia Ridge's PhD in digital humanities (Department of History, Open University) focuses on historians and scholarly crowdsourcing. Mia has published and presented widely on her key areas of interest including user experience design, human–computer interaction, open cultural data, audience engagement and crowdsourcing in the cultural heritage sector. While at the Science Museum, Mia held the first ever museum mashup competition, helped the Science Museum's Centenary Icons poll hit the front page of the BBC News, and organized the release of over 200,000 collections records as open data. Her edited volume, *Crowdsourcing our Cultural Heritage* (Ashgate) was published in 2014. She is Chair of the Museums Computer Group (MCG) and a member of the Executive Council of the Association for Computers and the Humanities (ACH).

Carli Spina

Carli Spina is the Emerging Technologies and Research Librarian at the Harvard Law School Library. She has published and presented on a variety of topics related to technology, librarianship and literature. Her interests include the use of technology in libraries, accessibility, user experience and teaching.

Graham Stone

Graham Stone is Information Resources Manager at the University of Huddersfield, UK, where he manages the library's information resources budget, including acquisitions, subscriptions and APC payments. He also manages the University Repository and University Press. Graham has been involved with a number of Jisc projects including the Library Analytics and Metrics Project (LAMP), Huddersfield Open Access Publishing and the OA best practice pathfinder project. He is co-author of OAWAL (Open Access Workflows for Academic Librarians) and TERMS (Techniques in E-Resources Management) with Jill Emery of Portland State University, UKSG Publications Officer and an *Insights* editorial board member. He is undertaking a doctorate at Huddersfield investigating the viability of the University Press as an OA publisher.

David Stuart

Dr David Stuart is a research fellow in the Centre for e-Research, King's College London, and an honorary research fellow in the Statistical Cybermetrics Research Group, University of Wolverhampton, from where he gained his PhD in webometrics. He is the author of two previous books published by Facet Publishing, *Facilitating Access to the Web of Data* (2011), and *Web Metrics for the Library and Information Professionals* (2014).

Elena Villaespesa

Elena Villaespesa works as Digital Analyst at Tate where she is responsible for managing digital analytics, which includes producing website, mobile and social media metrics reports and co-ordinating surveys to inform decision making, with the aim of improving user journeys across different digital platforms. Elena is also undertaking a PhD at the School of Museum Studies at the University of Leicester. Her research is about how museums can measure the impact and value of their social media activities.

Carrie E. Vass

As a Research Assistant at OCLC Research, Carrie E. Vass MA assists Senior Research Scientist Lynn Connaway on the activities: 'Cyber Synergy: Seeking Sustainability through Collaboration between Virtual Reference and Social Q&A Sites' and 'Visitors and Residents: What Motivates Engagement with the Digital Information Environment?'. She also assists Associate Research Scientist Ixchel Faniel on the 'E-Research and Data: Opportunities for Library Engagement' activity. She received both her BA and MA in communication studies from the University of North Carolina in Charlotte. Carrie's personal research interests include issues of power in popular culture, using a critical cultural lens to reveal, oftentimes, oppressive ideologies.

Acknowledgements

A book is a team sport. This is particularly the case with a book like this one, which relies so much on the examples and case studies provided by experts and practitioners from across the world. The case studies provide not just the in-depth and rich practical material for the book, but have also helped to guide and shape the overall feel of the book. So much of the credit for this book also belongs to the contributors.

I am particularly grateful to my publisher, Facet Publishing, both for the commissioning of this book and the stellar work of my editors, Jenni Hall and, most recently, Damian Mitchell. Not only have they reviewed the chapters as I drafted them, but they have managed to corral and encourage me so that, eventually, I handed in a final manuscript.

I'd also like to thank my colleagues in Jisc and the wider information, library and cultural communities. Their work, ideas and enthusiasm have inspired me in my work and directly led to the idea for this book. There are too many names to mention, but the innovative work taking place in the library and cultural heritage communities at present makes me confident that these communities will not just survive in the new information environment, but actively thrive.

Finally, I want to thank my family: specifically my wife, Jennie, for giving me the space and time I needed to write and for keeping everything going while I was furiously typing; and my children, Willow and Rowan, for providing the occasional interruption and light relief. And also my extended family – my mum, dad and brother – who are always there when needed.

Introduction: getting the measure of analytics and metrics

It seems that almost every aspect of our lives and the world around us is on the cusp of being transformed by the potential that data and the analysis of that data hold for the services and products we use and activities we undertake. Businesses and services are adopting analytics to help drive more informed decisions, to gain a better understanding of their customers and users and to make sense of the 'big data' created by all those interactions and actions. The potential appears limitless: from healthcare to education and from government to business.

Similarly, individuals are increasingly using analytics to help improve their performance and understanding of themselves. The 'quantified self' captures data from activities as diverse as running and sport, through to sleeping and general well-being. These popular apps and services enable the collection and analysis of data to help improve performance in whatever it is you're trying to achieve, whether running, sleeping or productivity at work.

The aim of this book is to explore the potential of analytics at an institutional and organizational level: how analytics can unlock a better understanding of your users, inform decision making and help drive new services.

Library analytics

Libraries, along with archives, museums and galleries, find themselves ideally placed to exploit the full potential of analytics.

Libraries, and the cultural sector more generally, have long been familiar with the potential of statistics and data for informing everything from service development to measurement of impact and value (both locally within the institution and nationally – and even internationally). The variety and scope of the data collected and generated by libraries and organizations such as museums and archives is significant: transactional data on catalogue searches, item check-outs, log-ins to online resources and services, swipes through the entrance gates; manually collected statistics on space usage, student satisfaction, external visitors to the library. The applications of the data are equally varied and overlapping, including management functions (collections development and management, usage statistics), impact (demonstrating value, benchmarking, improving learner outcomes) and improving services and meeting user requirements (recommendation services, collections management/development).

While this diversity in sources and applications is indicative of the importance of data to organizations like libraries, it also highlights the multi-faceted processes and practices for collecting and analysing the data. These practices are often unique to the local institution and its library and reflect both the accessibility of the data in its local systems and the specific uses and types of data that benefit that particular institution and its users. These local variations and challenges would by themselves be sufficient to make this a difficult landscape to traverse, but there are also significant external factors that conspire within the analytics space. Such complications include data access and ownership, formats and standards, privacy and ethical implications.

Maybe more critically, libraries and other institutions are beginning to question exactly what it is that they are measuring in the first place. There is a need to be clear about what is being measured, and why. Otherwise there is a very real risk that our measures become too simplistic or, worse, that we are simply measuring the wrong things: 'we look away from what we are measuring, and why we are measuring, and fixate on the measuring itself' (Crease, 2011).

The streetlight effect

Have you heard the parable of the man who lost his car keys? Walking from the office to his car in the dark, he fumbles for the keys to open the car door, but drops them somewhere in the gutter. The light in the gutter is poor and he searches on the pavement, where the light from the street light is brighter and it's easier to see.

He ends up walking home, unable to find his keys.

The implications of the streetlight effect (Freedman, 2010) are that we often look for answers where it is easiest to find information and data. The result is that we often end up focusing on the information and data that we find, rather than on our original questions. We are so busy searching in the light that we forget what we were looking for, or why it was important.

Much current work in libraries, archives, museums and galleries is looking to address this issue and make sure that we are asking the right questions in the beginning and finding new ways to expose and analyse the data that can contribute to answering these questions – and, indeed, help to refine and improve the questions themselves.

Much of what will follow in this book is a record of this 'analytics turn': a renewed concentration on the questions that we ask and how they evolve as the data we collect forms part of a feedback loop, informing both service developments and the reasons for measuring what's being measured, and improving the questions that we ask.

The challenges of getting analytics and metrics right are not insignificant, but their benefits to organizations like libraries and other cultural heritage institutions are compelling. This opportunity to begin measuring what really matters, is also one clearly recognized by the library community, but it is not unique to the library. The wider education and academic sectors recognize the importance of the right kind of metrics and analysis as a critical part of the services and systems they use and deliver.

For the libraries, the exploitation of learning and research analytics is likely to be an institutional priority for the foreseeable future.

Learning analytics

The potential and opportunities presented by the capture and analysis of data appear boundless. Nowhere is this sense of potential for analytics to transform felt more keenly than in the education sector.

In its 2013 edition the New Media Consortium Horizon Report for Higher Education (NMC, 2013) describes learning analytics as

> [the] field associated with deciphering trends and patterns from educational big data, or huge sets of student-related data, to further the advancement of a personalized, supportive system of higher education.

Put simply, learning analytics is concerned with understanding why some students may not be succeeding, what would contribute to their success and how and when interventions might be helpful. The vision is usually to create a more personalized and effective learning experience for students, and even for researchers. The benefits for learners are substantial, and they provide institutions with the opportunity to improve student satisfaction, as well as to enhance completion and retention rates. These are critical success factors for any academic institution.

Much of the current effort surrounding learning analytics is being put into assembling and organizing the disparate departments and services that might contribute to an institutional learning analytics strategy. This is no small task and represents significant institutional change in most cases. Furthermore, much current discussion is around how learning analytics can move beyond a simplistic approach to learning, to look at performance beyond the confines of the classroom.

The library has a clear role to play in this larger analytics picture, contributing both its data and analytics experiences and its leadership and expertise, in effectively collecting and analysing data for the benefit of students and in delivering more effective and efficient services.

About this book

This book will provide libraries and cultural heritage institutions with an overview of some of the main themes surrounding analytics and the development of metrics. Each of the major themes is accompanied by a series of short, practical case studies describing the development of services or outlining current research and practice in that area. It is hoped that the book will be of use to both managers and library directors in helping them to think about the challenges and implications of analytics in their library or institution, as well as to practitioners who are currently working with analytics or want to learn more. This is ultimately a practical book: you should be able to read the case studies and apply some (or all) of their content to your current role and your library or institution.

Chapter summaries
1 Library data: big and small

This chapter explores the definitions of these increasingly popular terms and provides a clear understanding of the differences between them and of the kinds of opportunities that they present to libraries and cultural heritage institutions. While big data captures much of the headlines, it is of little use if we can't get the 'small data' of our systems and services up to scratch.

2 Data-driven collections management

This chapter delves into some of the developments currently taking place in the library sector to exploit the potential of analytics so as to help drive informed decisions about the purchase of materials, usage and collections management and opportunities to extend the impact of the library into new domains.

3 Using data to demonstrate library impact and value

Analytics are increasingly being used to uncover new insights and demonstrate new types of value and impact for libraries and their institutions.

This chapter explores some of the current opportunities that institutions are exploiting through the use of analytics, and the innovative services and tools they are developing.

4 Going beyond the numbers: using qualitative research to transform the library user's experience

While much of the buzz around data and analytics is inevitably about the quantitative 'big data', the role of qualitative data in informing decisions is critical. This chapter explores the many ways in which institutions and researchers are capturing this kind of data and the kinds of insights it is providing.

5 Web and social media metrics for the cultural heritage sector

This chapter explores the potential of web analytics for cultural heritage institutions. The increasingly social nature of the web, and in particular the sharing and discovery of content and resources, makes this is a critical area for any cultural institution to understand.

6 Understanding and managing the risks of analytics

This chapter explores the legal and ethical risks of analytics and provides best practice and practical examples for how they can be met and managed.

7 Conclusion: towards a data-driven future?

A peek into the future: given the current work and developments that are taking place within cultural heritage institutions and organizations, how might such developments change the cultural landscape over the next five to ten years? What might a data-driven future look like?

Analytics and metrics: a brief note on definitions

Before we go any further it seems worthwhile to pause briefly and explore the two critical terms that will be used throughout this book: *analytics* and *metrics*. I will not provide an in-depth discussion of the terms but, rather, make sure that we all begin with a similar understanding of the terms. This is also a useful way to introduce some of the complexities and controversies of the two terms.

Analytics

Analytics is the *discovery* and *communication* of meaningful patterns in data (Wikipedia: en.wikipedia.org/wiki/Analytics). Importantly, analytics is about analysing data to uncover information and knowledge (discovery) and using these insights to make recommendations (communication) for specific actions or interventions. The term 'actionable insights' is often used specifically to describe the kind of information that analytics should provide: information that leads directly to an action or actions.

The communication aspect of analytics is often done through visualizations: taking complex patterns of data and representing them in a visually meaningful way that informs specific actions. A good example of a well-known analytics service is Google Analytics, which provides analysis on website data, such as the number of people visiting a site, where they come from geographically and so on, and delivers this analysis via different visualizations on a web dashboard.

Metrics

In the context of this book and of its use in the analysis of data, metrics means the criteria against which something is *measured*. A more formal definition is provided by the Oxford English Dictionary as: 'a system or standard of measurement; a criterion or set of criteria stated in quantifiable terms' (OED, 2001).

If you are a salesperson, the number of sales you make in a given period or the amount of positive feedback you receive may be the specific metric against which you are measured. By using that data as a benchmark you can make an informed decision about your performance as a salesperson. Metrics can also be applied to much more complex areas, such as bibliometrics, which seeks to apply mathematical and statistical methods to the analysis of research outputs and literature to measure citations of articles, for example. Bibliometrics is increasingly used to explore the impact of a specific field of research, and even the impact of individual research papers.

As with the streetlight effect described above, there is often an inevitable bias towards the types of data that can be captured rather than the data that *should* be captured. Indeed, the increasingly controversial topic of journal article impacts and how they are measured provides an example of the potential problems that an inappropriate application of metrics can have on education and, in particular, in research.

References

Crease, R. (2011) Measurement and its Discontents, *New York Times*, 22 October.
Freedman, H. David (2010) Why Scientific Studies are So Often Wrong: the

Streetlight Effect, *Discover*, July/August 2010.

New Media Consortium (2013) *NMC Horizon Report: 2013 Higher Education Report*, www.nmc.org/publications/2013-horizon-report-higher-ed.

Oxford English Dictionary (2001) www.oed.com.

Library data: big and small

Chapter overview

As our cultural heritage institutions find themselves collecting and storing more and more of the usage data created by patrons' and users' interactions with the systems and services of the library, archive, museum or gallery, so there is an increase in the potential to extract value from this largely unstructured data.

This chapter will use the concepts of 'big' and 'small' data as a way to explore some of the analytics developments in academic and cultural heritage institutions. Rather than simply assuming the promises of big data and the desire to collect and analyse more and more data, small data provides us with a balance, a refocus on the localized, contextual and manageable data and can provide a fertile environment for the development of data analysis at ever greater scale; from individual institutions to groups or entire sectors and from individual data sets through to multiple and disparate datasets.

The chapter provides an overview of two early-stage analytics developments that promise to show how we can use both small and big data to shape our services and user interactions with them, both at an organizational level and at a sector level (although the case studies do not use the concepts of big and small data in articulating the work they do). The two case studies featured are:

- CASE STUDY 1.1 Nurse, R., *The potential of data to inform personalized recommendations at the Open University Library* (The Open University), p. 5
- CASE STUDY 1.2 Showers, B., *Library 'big' data: developing a shared analytics service for academic libraries* (Jisc), p. 14

But before we explore the potential of big and small data for libraries and cultural heritage organizations it is worth briefly unpacking these terms and attempting to arrive at a definition for each.

Defining big and small data

Big data is commonly thought of as a collection of datasets that are so large and complex that they are difficult to process using standard database management and processing tools. Typically, the term is applied in areas such as physics or astronomy, where the data collected from experiments and observations is enormous and the burden of storage, analysis and visualization is tremendous. However, we might also understand big data as being a quantity of data that is beyond the usual capacity of an organization to handle. In this sense, big data applies to organizations in all fields, not just those usually associated with the collection and analysis of large datasets.

The hype or promise of big data is about the potential for insights to be gleaned from analysing these datasets at a hitherto unknown scale; from analysing Google search queries to understand the spread and distribution of influenza, through to the delivery of personalized services, even medicine based not just on an analysis of your personal data but on a comparison with everyone else's.

But the concept of big data remains a contested one, in terms both of big data as a methodology or approach to gaining insight and understanding and of the slightly dystopian implications (as well as, some would argue, the utopian possibilities) of such an approach to data.

In contrast both to the scale of the data and the hyperbole associated with big data, we might introduce a companion concept: small data. Rufus Pollock, of the Open Knowledge Foundation, describes small data as 'the amount of data you can conveniently store and process on a single machine, and in particular, a high-end laptop or server' (Pollock, 2013). Pollock explicitly contrasts small data with big data: it's the data you can manage locally, using your everyday tools. What's important here is that the data originates from a localized context in which it might be enriched and improved, analysed and acted upon. From this localized, distributed and context-rich source, any larger aggregation or analysis across datasets rests on two very important foundations:

1   an immediate, local context for the data, with potential for a perspective across a larger whole
2   an ability to share the data and make its analysis a mass-participation activity; the opportunities to open up the data and make it accessible are much better at the local level.

If analytics depends increasingly on big data, then big data depends on small data to provide meaningful insights. To understand the importance of the local management and flow of data it is worth briefly exploring some of the emerging examples of cultural heritage big data.

Small and big data in libraries

As the hardware and infrastructure for managing and analysing (big) data decreases in cost and complexity, so there is a renewed focus on the institutions' ability to better understand their local data flows and to capture and export the usage and interaction data that circulates throughout their various systems and services.

This increased understanding of the institutions' local data has given rise in the last few years to some interesting experiments and developments in cultural heritage big data. In his blog, Lorcan Dempsey (Dempsey, 2012) highlights some examples from the US Library of Congress, including:

- the Digging into Data project, which utilized 5 million newspaper pages, imaged with OCR, for data mining
- the 5 billion files of different types in a single institutional web archive
- requests for research access to over 50 billion Tweets for linguistic analysis, analysis of geographic spread of news stories and so on.

There are similar examples in the UK, including the British Library. Most recently, in 2014 the British Library announced a collaboration with University College London's Computer Science and Digital Humanities departments as part of a big data experiment to open up the digital collections of the British Library for the benefit of arts and humanities researchers (British Library, 2014).

Internationally, an increasing number of services are being developed expressly to begin to realize the potential of localized data aggregated and analysed at a much greater scale than was previously imagined.

The University of Pennsylvania, for example, has developed Metridoc, which is described as 'an extensible framework that supports library assessment and analytics, using a wide variety of activity data collected from heterogeneous sources' (Jisc, 2012). The architecture of the service means that it is able to collect data from disparate systems across the campus and aggregate it into a large data repository. It can also be scaled to capture data from new systems as they are implemented locally, thus ensuring that it is not tied by the current systems and processes of the institution. Metridoc aims to enable a big data-like analysis of data across the university (from administration systems to the library), and its architecture is specifically designed to realize the potential of all those small, discrete datasets from across the campus.

This subtle distinction between focusing on local data flows and the exploitation and analysis of this data at ever greater scales is particularly evident in the academic and cultural heritage sectors. This stands in contrast to the largely commercial hype around big data and the focus on analysis at an enormous scale. This dual focus on big and small data, as exemplified in the cultural heritage sector, is an approach which has a number of important and urgent advantages:

1 **The combination of small and big data approaches provides a more robust basis for data analysis.**
   As we have already discussed, small data provides the meaningful context for any data which is aggregated at scale. It ensures that the analysis is meaningful, taking into account factors which might otherwise be missed. It also helps to ensure that there is a local focus on data, on collecting and producing data of better quality and on making it accessible, and recognizes that it is the data which ultimately provides the basis for the development of new applications, systems and services.

2 **The dual approach enables an explicit focus on the data, not on the services or systems that interrogate and analyse the data.**
   There is a shift in emphasis, away from the primacy of systems and applications and towards a data-centric approach in which the data and the data flows become the centre of attention. This is important for a number of reasons: it stops us from thinking in data silos, where data is inaccessible to other systems; effort is put into improving both data flows and data quality; and this data helps to feed the systems and services that depend upon it to offer the kinds of functionality that users require.

3 **It exploits the significant decrease in the cost of tools, services and infrastructure for storing and analysing big data that has occurred over the past few years.**
   Increasingly, therefore, we do not need to expend our energy on the development of bespoke infrastructure or tools. It makes more sense for the cultural heritage and library sectors to collaborate wherever they can share the costs of infrastructure, and to identify shared opportunities for reducing the costs of big data tools and storage. The areas that do require attention are those associated with small data and local data quality, making that data open and available to other systems and services and, critically, the skills and expertise of staff.

4 **It develops data literacy and capabilities locally.**
   The argument so far has largely been that there are significant advantages for institutions and organizations in adopting a small-data approach to data and analytics and establishing this as the basis for any subsequent scaling up. It is also the case that the costs associated with big data storage and infrastructure are decreasing, so it makes no sense for individual institutions to use their resources locally to develop big data infrastructures. Instead, it makes sense to spend resources on small data. This primarily means improving the data literacy of staff and increasing their skills to work with data. By collecting data of high quality, improving its flow across systems and having skilled staff to analyse it, the local institution is in a position to really benefit from the potential of large-scale data analytics to effect meaningful change locally.

It is probably now worth looking at some examples of initiatives that help to demonstrate the opportunities of exploiting data at both the small and big scales.

As the following two case studies make clear, there are opportunities for institutions both at the local, institutional level (the small-data level) and at the national, shared or sector level (the big-data level) to reap advantages from data and its analysis. At the local level a better understanding of the data and its flows across our systems can enable systems to provide a better service and experience for users. At the national level – where we begin to get close to notions of big data – there are opportunities for institutions to collaborate on infrastructure and tools, while gaining previously impossible types of insight into users and collections, and to enable new forms of experience for users. What these case studies highlight, more than anything else, is that the data environment is changing rapidly and inexorably, and that what has worked well in the past may no longer be appropriate in the future. Indeed, the future may need to be protected from the past!

CASE STUDY 1.1

The potential of data to inform personalized recommendations at the Open University Library
Richard Nurse, Open University

Introduction
'Customers who viewed this also viewed' (Amazon), 'People who listen to this artist are also listening to this artist' (Spotify), the most popular news stories shared (BBC News). Wherever you go on the web there is a very good chance that you will encounter some form of recommendation generated by activity data. Increasingly, that recommendation is also being informed by your behaviour. In other words, it is personalized, and whether that personalization is driven by the music you have listened to or the products you have bought, your experience of the web is likely to be different, maybe in a subtle way, from someone else's.

Whether we realize it or not, user expectations of library systems are nowadays being set by those web-scale companies such as Amazon and Google (Knott et al., 2007; Brophy and Bawden, 2005). Library users have now moved beyond wondering why library systems don't look like Amazon, Google or Facebook, to expecting that our library search systems *will* work in pretty much the same way as Google. For many of our library users, Google defines what a search system should be like, and they don't see why library systems would be any different.

Yet library systems look very different from our web-scale competitors. Traditional library catalogues typically lack activity data-driven features or recommendations, and examples of such tools are still remarkably rare. Early work, in projects such as the Jisc-funded MOSAIC (Making our Scholarly Activity Information Count) project (Sero Consulting, 2010) and work by Dave Pattern at the University of Huddersfield (Pattern, 2009) have explored this landscape extensively. Yet, this type of exploitation of user activity data is still far from mainstream.

Although one supplier, ExLibris, with its product bX, now offers recommendations and most-popular articles based on mining activity data, this type of feature isn't universal in either the current generation of discovery tools or the new generation of library services platforms. Yet, libraries are often sitting on significant repositories of activity data – from their circulation systems, access control systems, PC booking systems, log files of catalogues and discovery systems, and from the systems that manage access to the burgeoning range of digital content. Yet much of this data remains unused in the majority of institutions for any purpose other than to produce statistics or performance indicators. The revolution of Web 2.0 that exploits the trail generated as a by-product of service use remains largely unused by most library systems.

Background

As a distance-learning institution, the Open University (OU) Library Services has some unique features when compared with a traditional, campus-based library. With over 200,000 students enrolled at the University there is potentially a large pool of data relating to student interactions with the library. But students rarely, if ever, visit the main OU campus in Milton Keynes, so there is no significant library lending activity, nor student PC use, nor student gate-count data to draw upon. However, students do interact with the OU library through their use of library resources that are embedded at point of use in their courses' virtual learning-environment websites. We also have the advantage of a single sign-on solution, and have moved to providing most of our online access using OCLC's EZproxy authentication and access software. This interaction generates a large amount of activity data, which is recorded in the EZproxy log files.

At the OU, the quality of the online experience is vital, and forms a significant element of a student's engagement with the University and the library. In 2011 we had just implemented a new discovery system from EBSCO to try to provide more of a 'Google-like' library search experience. Because student expectations of the online world were now being driven by the experiences offered by such web services as Amazon and Facebook, the

OU was keen to explore the role that 'Amazon-like' recommendations could play in improving the student experience.

What we set out to do and our approach

The OU was fortunate to receive funding as part of Jisc's Activity Data programme during 2011 for a six-month project that we called RISE – Recommendations Improve the Search Experience (www.open.ac.uk/blogs/RISE). For this project we started with a hypothesis: 'That recommender systems can enhance the student experience in new generation e-resource discovery services'. RISE proposed a short programme of work to create a recommender service and to show recommendations to users through a search interface using the API for our discovery system. The project also looked at users' views of the value of recommendations and used Google Analytics to track use of the tool and the recommendations.

Project activities revolved around five distinct elements:

- the data, where was it, what was it and what could be done with it
- the interface, building prototype search tools
- the issues
- the recommendations, what type and how
- the user perspective.

A small project team was set up, with a project manager and some time from specialist staff across the library, and a programmer was brought in to do the development work. As the project progressed we blogged regularly about what we were doing, what issues we encountered and what we were discovering.

Data

We started by exploring the data that was available in the EZproxy log files in more detail. Broadly, the content included date/timestamp information, session information, referrer and request data and, importantly for our plan to create recommendations, a user ID in the form of an OU computer user-account name. We had been collecting log files for a few months, with a view to carrying out this project, but generally the log files have been kept only to assist with resolving licence breach issues. One of the important considerations when working with activity data is to ensure that the data is kept, and not destroyed. The Data Protection Act (1998) Principle 5 relating to the retention of personal data requires that 'Personal data processed for any purpose or purposes shall not be kept for longer than is necessary for that purpose or those purposes' (Information Commissioner's Office). There can be a tension between the desire to keep useful data and the legal requirement to state and comply with data retention schedules. Making use of data to drive recommender services or to allow users to see the library resources that they have accessed can provide a justification for retaining data. The relatively new discipline of learning analytics faces many of the same challenges around data and how it can or should be used (Siemens, 2013).

Our next steps were to design a database in MySQL to store the log file data and to work out how to parse the log files. By this stage we had begun to understand the limitations of the log file content and realized that the log file data alone would not be sufficient for our purposes. Essentially, the log file data became the starting-point and the approach that we took was to match key elements of the log file against other data sources to enhance the content of the database.

The user ID allows us to identify the type of user (whether student or staff, for example), as well as their course or faculty affiliation. The request in the log file was used as a way to acquire more complete bibliographic data. One of the challenges that we faced was how to get from a URL to something that would be useful to a user when presented in the interface: if I'm given a recommendation I need some form of recognizable description, some bibliographic data such as the author, article title and journal title. That turned out to be difficult because, although we were able to use the discovery-solution API to retrieve bibliographic data we were prevented by our licence agreement from storing that metadata locally. That meant that we had to take the approach of using the discovery metadata as a way to get data from Crossref (www.crossref.org) that we were allowed to store within the recommendations database. An illustration of the recommender database improvement flow is shown in Figure 1.1.

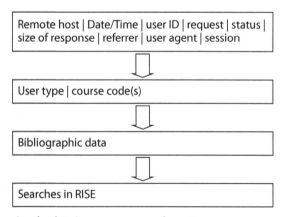

Remote host | Date/Time | user ID | request | status | size of response | referrer | user agent | session

User type | course code(s)

Bibliographic data

Searches in RISE

Figure 1.1 *Improving the data in your recommender system*

The log file data also offered session IDs and date/timestamps which were useful in helping to form other types of recommendations of the type 'people who looked at resource A also looked at resource B'. One final type of data was added to the database by storing search terms used by users as they interacted with the system.

Interface and the issues

We designed a simple user interface using the EBSCO Discovery API to act as the base for recommendations to be displayed to users. The search interface had a simple search box with Keyword, Title and Author search options that allowed users to search the discovery system in a way that was very similar to how it was implemented on the library's website. In this short-term experimental project we wanted to ensure that users weren't distracted by elements that were peripheral to what we were trying to test. The user interface used our standard institutional website style-sheet and users logged in through the institutional access and authentication system (Figure 1.2). We also built a cut-down version of the search system as a Google Gadget.

RISE also investigated issues around privacy and anonymity. As part of a strand of projects looking at activity data it was particularly useful to be able to compare notes with and take advice from others working in this area. RISE eventually developed a separate privacy policy that was linked from the user interface and also adopted an opt-out feature to allow users to flag that they wanted their data to be removed from the recommendations database.

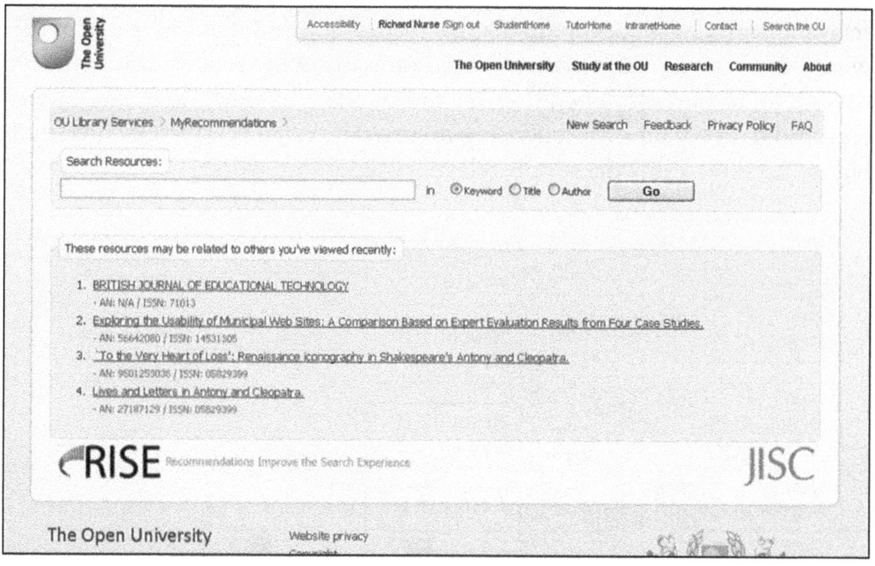

Figure 1.2 *RISE user interface*

What type of activity data-driven recommendations were made?

The data that you are able to collect or generate determines the types of recommendation that you can make. In our case three types of recommendation were possible:

- Course based: *'Users on my course accessed these resources.'* These were based on knowing the course the user was studying and then listing the resources viewed by users on that course. These recommendations were presented immediately the user logged in to the search interface.
- Enquiry based: *'Users of this or a similar search term accessed these resources.'* These recommendations were generated from the search terms used in the search interface by identifying from the log files the resources that were subsequently accessed. These recommendations were shown to users once they had entered a search term and appeared at the bottom of the results page.
- Expansion based: *'These resources may be related to others you've viewed recently.'* These recommendations were derived by implying a relationship to resources viewed sequentially. Thus there is an implied relationship between two resources viewed one after another and there is assumed to be a relatively high chance that they might be relevant to someone viewing one or other of the resources. These recommendations were made as soon as the user logged in and also relied on tracking the search history of users within the system.

To make some sense of the recommendations we also created a simple relevancy-ranking algorithm to display the recommendations in an order that would be more useful. This was based on scoring the relationship between users and resources, depending on the number of times that the pattern reoccurred. Every time a relationship occurred its value was incremented by 1. Figure 1.3 shows how the simple relevancy algorithm works.

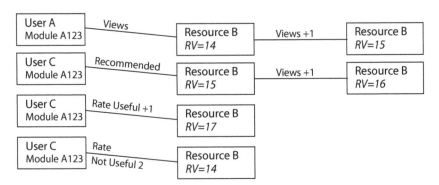

Figure 1.3 *A simple relevancy algorithm*

We also put in place a simple rating system for users to flag recommendations as useful or not useful. Scores from the rating system contributed to the overall value and this was used to determine the order in which recommendations appeared on screen. Thus, recommendations that appeared, were selected and were rated as useful would stay at the top of the recommendations. This potential for reinforcing recommendations is one of the criticisms of recommendations, in that they can tend to perpetuate a narrow range of resources which, because they are being recommended, are therefore viewed, and so they are recommended, and so on.

Users' perspective

To find out from users whether they found recommendations to be useful we used a survey, a series of 11 interviews with students, some questions during our discovery system focus groups and Google Analytics. In the survey two-thirds of the 26 respondents judged the recommendations to be useful and 61% saw the recommendations as being relevant. When we asked about the three different types of recommendations we saw quite similar results, with the course recommendations being slightly less useful (Table 1.1).

Table 1.1 *Survey results for the value of different types of recommendations*

Type	Very useful	Quite useful	Slightly useful	Not useful	Not sure
Course	31%	15%	15%	39%	0%
Enquiry	47%	20%	0%	33%	0%
Expansion	45%	22%	0%	22%	11%

During the focus group sessions there was a general agreement that recommendations were useful, but both undergraduates and postgraduates were keen to know the provenance of the recommendations. Undergraduates were keen to get recommendations from high-performing students, for example.

All of the students interviewed said that they liked the idea of getting recommendations on library resources, and 100% said they preferred course-related recommendations – mainly because these would be seen to be the most relevant and lead to a quick find:

> 'I take a really operational view you know, I'm on here, I want to get the references for this particular piece of work, and those are the people that are most likely to be doing a similar thing that I can use.'
>
> Postgraduate education student

There was also an appreciation that recommendations might give a more diverse picture of the literature on a topic:

'I think it is useful because you run out of things to actually search for.... You don't always think to look in some of the other journals ... there's so many that you can't know them all. So I think that is a good idea. You might just think "oh I'll try that". It might just bring something up that you'd not thought of.'

Postgraduate psychology student

'People using similar search terms often viewed' was rated as useful by some interviewees who lacked confidence in using library databases:

'Yes, I would definitely use that because my limited knowledge of the library might mean that other people were using slightly different ways of searching and getting different results.'

Undergraduate English literature student

Helpfully, students also suggested some improvements, including making the recommendations more obvious and indicating their popularity, e.g. 'X percentage of people on your module recommended A' or '10 people viewed this and 5 found it useful'. They also suggested showing the currency of the recommendations. Something that was recommended a year ago might be of less interest than something recommended this week.

One of the things that we were able to do with Google Analytics was to track which of the different types of recommendations were being used. We needed to be slightly cautious with this, as different numbers of recommendations were shown at different times, but one of the particularly interesting facts that emerged was that the first two recommendations were far more likely to be chosen. The first recommendation was nine times more likely to be chosen than the third, and the second recommendation was six times more likely to be chosen than the third. That is something to bear in mind when designing recommender systems.

Conclusions

The RISE project identified three big lessons for us about making use of activity data from online resource use.

Firstly, if you want to make use of activity data, then you need to make sure that you retain it for an appropriate period of time. Our EZproxy log files were routinely destroyed after a few months because they were not being used. Using the data to provide recommendations provides a justification for keeping the data (but you still need to ensure that you think about when to delete this data from the recommendations system).

Secondly, although you can make recommendations from proxy log files it isn't particularly straightforward. All that the log files give you as a recommendation is a relationship that says 'a user looked at this resource and then looked at that resource'. To make other types of recommendations you need to treat the log file as the first link in a chain of data. You must use the user's ID to find out which course they are on (to make the recommendation 'Students on your course are looking at these resources'), and save the search terms they use in your systems (to make the recommendation 'People who searched for this subject looked at these resources').

Finally, you need bibliographic data, and it isn't always easy to get that from the log files or from the systems you use. And when you get it you can't always store it locally, due to licensing restrictions. You need article titles, journal titles and dates so that you can show users some details that will allow them to judge if the recommendations will be useful to them.

Overall, our users liked the idea of recommendations and would expect to see them in our systems. They may sometimes want to be sure about the provenance of recommendations, and could see this as a feature that would be useful to them.

More recently we've started to explore aspects of search functionality. Our MACON project (Mobilising Academic Content Online, www.open.ac. uk/blogs/macon) developed a mobile search interface and explored the value of showing recent search terms and recent resources viewed. We've also looked in detail, with students, at the wider context of personalization in relation to an online library. Surveying our student panel has allowed us to see how popular recommender-type services are in comparison to other personalized services (see, for example, www.lmschange.info/blog/2013/03/personalisation-at-the-ou). Students gave the highest ranking to bookmarking services that would allow them to manage their library resources, alongside recommendations of new resources and relevant skills-development material. This may provide an insight into the preoccupations of students whose study resources are increasingly digital in nature.

It's clear from this work that students like the idea of taking more control of their library data, so we have followed this up by working with a group of students as co-designers to specify a My Recent resources tool that lets students view the library resources they have used. This programme of work is now informing the development of new prototype library search tools for OU students.

I'd like to thank the Project Manager, Elizabeth Mallett, the RISE developer, Paul Grand, and the staff and students at the OU who contributed to this project. I'd also like to thank the team from the Activity Data Synthesis project and Jisc for their work on this project strand.

Library 'big data': developing a shared analytics service for academic libraries

Ben Showers, Jisc

Introduction

Libraries are no strangers to the potential of data. Indeed, it is data that drives the systems and services that libraries deliver to their users, from the metadata that enables discovery and access to content, to the management and transactional data that (a) helps to ensure that library collections and services meet the requirements of students and researchers and (b) demonstrates the value that the library delivers to the host institution.

Yet, identifying, collecting and analysing data that will help to drive service development and demonstrate impact is not straightforward. Indeed, three key factors conspire to make this task increasingly difficult.

1   Cost versus value: Collecting the data can be resource intensive, often requiring far more time to identify and collect the data than is spent in acting on it.
2   Increasing volumes: The sheer amount of data and data sources is increasing. As the business of the library becomes increasingly digital and more processes are automated, the library is confronted with trying to make sense of voluminous amounts of (often unstructured) data.
3   Data beyond the library: To develop effective services and systems, and to demonstrate value to the wider institution, the data that libraries require is located not just in their local systems but also across the campus and in external aggregations.

The resource implications, as well as the sheer amount of data, make the task of analysing and acting on the data potentially more difficult; especially when library budgets and resources are already pushed to the limit.

These challenges, however, have not inhibited the increasing strategic desire of libraries to be able to make use of this data both to inform the development of existing and new services and to explore ways to demonstrate the library's value to and impact on the institution and its students and researchers.

An appetite for analytics

Libraries are actively engaged in exploring the potential of analytics. This is visibly the case in the increasingly rich landscape of both UK and international activities exploring ways to exploit and maximize the potential of library and institutional data.

The Library Impact Data Project (LIDP), led by the University of Huddersfield (see further resources section at the end of this chapter), looked at data from over 33,000 undergraduate students from across eight universities to examine the validity of the hypothesis that there was a statistical significance across a number of universities between library activity data (specifically book issues and electronic resource usage) and student attainment (Stone and Ramsden, 2013).

The conclusions of the project supported the hypothesis and demonstrated the (non-causal) relationship between library usage and student success.

The work at Huddersfield as part of the Jisc Activity Data programme (www.activitydata.org) exemplifies some of the institutional-level activity around analytics. This work includes both a focus on library impact and value and an interest in projects looking at personalization and recommendation services, as at the Open University (see Case Study 1.1 above) and in Manchester Information and Associated Services (Mimas) at the University of Manchester (www.activitydata.org/SALT). This local, institutional activity is also complemented by the national, shared services that have been developed to provide easy access to some of this transactional and usage data, including, for example, the Journal Usage Statistics Portal (JUSP, www. jusp.mimas.ac.uk), the Institutional Repository Usage Statistics (IRUS, www. irus.mimas.ac.uk), and Copac Collections Management (CCM, http://copac. ac.uk/innovations/collections-management).

Building on this fertile environment of experimentation and service development in library data, Jisc, the University of Huddersfield and Mimas wanted to explore the sector's appetite for analytics in general, and the potential demand for a shared data-analytics service in particular. In the autumn of 2012 a survey was distributed to all UK academic library directors, which resulted in 66 responses.

Of those who replied 96% confirmed that they would want automated provision of analytics, demonstrating the relationship between student attainment and library usage within in their institution, and 94.6% wanted to benchmark their data with other institutions. Further, 87.7% were interested in the richer data that was used as part of the second phase of LIDP, e.g. discipline, age, year, nationality and grade.

There was also a strong willingness to share a broad range of data; however, only 47% institutions wanted to be identified, and the majority (91%) preferred some kind of anonymization, e.g. to be identified by Jisc band.

When respondents were asked if this was likely to become a top priority in the next five years, the evidence from the survey was clear, with almost all saying it was either a top priority (39) or important but not essential (21). More

on the results of the survey can be found here: http://jisclamp.mimas.
ac.uk/2013/04/library-analytics-community-survey-results.

The key strategic drivers for the use of library analytics that the library
survey identified were, perhaps unsurprisingly:

1   enhancing the student experience
2   demonstrating value for money
3   supporting research excellence.

With a set of clear, near-term strategic drivers for institutions, a rich library
data/analytics landscape and the support of the Society of College, National
and University Libraries (SCONUL) and Research Libraries UK (RLUK), it
was agreed there was compelling evidence of the need and desire for a shared
library analytics service.

Library Analytics and Metrics Project

Running from January 2013 to May 2015, the Library Analytics and Metrics
Project (LAMP) aims to develop a prototype shared library analytics service
for, and in collaboration with, UK academic libraries. By May 2015 the LAMP
prototype will deliver a data dashboard enabling libraries to capitalize on the
many types of data they capture in day-to-day activities and will support the
improvement and development of new services and demonstrate value and
impact in new ways across an institution, in line with the three key strategic
drivers highlighted above.

As LAMP begins its second phase, it is clear that there are three core
components to the work so far, and to the work to develop the prototype
service by March 2015. These are:

1   analysis: how the data is meaningfully displayed to users
2   community: the role of the library community in helping develop, shape
    and deliver LAMP
3   data: the disparate institutional datasets that will be ingested and
    analysed by the service.

Data

LAMP will use the opportunities of scale to access a much larger number of
datasets, analysable both at the local, institutional level and at the shared,
above-campus level. In both cases it is hoped to gain new insights, such as on
national usage patterns, and to enhance services and functionality for
institutions, such as benchmarking and personalization.

Specifically, this means that LAMP will ingest and normalize various institutional datasets, including UCAS data (data from the Universities and Colleges Admissions Service in the UK, which is LAMP's primary source for individual student data such as age, gender, course and so forth), library loans data, e-resource logins, library gate counts and examination data (student attainment/records). Even with the relatively limited amount of data LAMP aims to collect, there are still a number of cultural and technical challenges, such as that these datasets are often stored in different systems and are owned by different departments. This conspires to make their collection and aggregation difficult. While the project will require a minimum number of core datasets to provide a certain level of service, it will ultimately need to provide back to institutions a view (or views) on the datasets they were able to supply. LAMP, as a service, must recognize that institutional access to different data types and datasets is not uniform but will vary widely between institutions.

In the longer term, however, it will become increasingly important for institutions to be able to track the 'journey' of the student from prospect to alumnus, if they are to be able to offer the kinds of experience that will quickly become the norm in education. This will make it critical to access more datasets across the campus. Also, while at the prototype stage LAMP utilizes one-off anonymized datasets, the need to track over time means that the project (or institutions) will need to find ways of using anonymized identifiers that can track the same student over the three or more years of their course. As the prototype develops into a service this will become a critical challenge to address.

Its work with six institutional data providers (see the LAMP blog for further details of the partners, http://jisclamp.mimas.ac.uk/team-and-partners) is enabling the project to explore exactly these kinds of difficulties. At present much of the burden of contributing data sits with the institutions and libraries, but as LAMP develops from a prototype to a service this burden will need to shift onto the service.

One area that LAMP is actively exploring to reduce the institutional burden of submitting data is to ingest other, national datasets, some of which may include the local datasets required by LAMP. The prototype LAMP architecture is therefore built around Application Programming Interfaces (APIs). LAMP will use an API to deliver data to its own user interface (the dashboard) as well as to consume external data from other APIs and sources. This approach will also allow LAMP users to access more data, and display the results of the analysis via their own applications, if they prefer to do so.

Those other services and aggregations include JUSP, IRUS, the Higher Education Statistics Agency and SCONUL, for example. These will provide a potential route to automating data consumption, and enable the sharing of appropriate data with other services and integrating processes where possible. Similarly, LAMP will itself become a national dataset which will enable the development of applications such as benchmarking and performance measurement. Already, for example, the prototype can tell whether the output described is statistically significant or not – something not easily achieved at the institutional level.

The ability to bring together more datasets from more sources opens up the possibility of being able to respond to difficult questions to which institutions want to know the answer. Indeed, it offers the possibility of asking entirely new questions.

But so much of this potential functionality will depend on the ability of the LAMP service to be able to offer *meaningful* answers in response to the kinds of questions that librarians and others will want to ask of it.

Analysis

For LAMP, much of the first year of development has been about addressing the challenges of obtaining and 'cleaning' the necessary institutional datasets. Much of this was behind-the-scenes development, and in close collaboration with the contributing libraries. But, while data represents the bedrock of the LAMP prototype, it is the service's ability to provide a 'view' or analysis of that data that really matters.

The project is now at the stage of exploring how the data is presented to the user and understanding the division between how much the service can provide and how much analysis needs to be performed by the user.

In order to explore these questions the project has developed, in conjunction with the Jisc community advisory group, a number of user and job stories to get a clear sense of how libraries might want to use the data, the kinds of things they would want it to tell them and what they would want to do with it. Maybe more importantly, the project has also developed an 'ugly prototype' (as it has become affectionately known) to test with potential users the kinds of analysis they would want to be able to do on the data (and indeed to show the kinds of data that LAMP can provide).

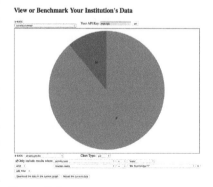

An example of the kinds of data LAMP can currently provide is shown in Figure 1.4. This simple pie chart

Figure 1.4
Example of the kind of data delivered by the LAMP 'ugly prototype': loans activity for a specific subject, broken down by gender

demonstrates loans activity among students studying for a bachelor's degree in Psychology, broken down by gender.

At first glance it would appear female students borrow more books than their male counterparts – or do they? Are there simply more women studying that discipline? Already, even the most straightforward graph begins to throw up questions for anyone viewing the data. Indeed, it may be that there are other, more important or interesting questions we should be asking of this particular set of data, such as what the differences are between full-time and part-time students and their book borrowing habits, and how they break down between genders.

Is it enough to provide just this particular graph? The question for LAMP is 'what story is this data actually telling?'

The ability to misinterpret or take the data out of context is a potentially important consideration, and it is beholden on LAMP to ensure that it does all it can to mitigate the risks inherent in the complexities of data.

The ugly prototype and collection of job stories have provided the project with a starting-point from which to begin exploring these kinds of questions and to understand the requirements both for the visualizations the service provides, and the for data literacy of the users who are interacting with the service.

The final stages of the project will be exploring these questions explicitly and developing the prototype with librarians to refine the way the data is described via the interface. As with the data, the analysis aspects of LAMP require a close relationship with the library community to enable the project to test and refine the prototype over the coming months.

Community

For LAMP, the academic community – and specifically the academic library community – is the critical partner in ensuring the success of the eventual LAMP prototype and service.

From accessing the institutional data through to developing, testing and refining the user and job stories, the project has relied on its Community Advisory and Planning group. This group of engaged experts has helped to shape much of the work so far and is helping to ensure that the LAMP prototype now under development will meet the needs of libraries and institutions.

Importantly, this group and its subset of data contributors is willingly taking upon itself a significant amount of the burden in order to help the project access the relevant data and build the prototype interface. As described already, accessing the data is no simple feat, and negotiating across institutions is a considerable task.

Ultimately, LAMP needs to work with the library community to ensure that it is able to deliver the analysis and information that will enable institutions to act upon what really matters to their students, researchers and users. Working with the library community becomes more critical as the project begins to develop its prototype service and seeks to engage more institutions in both testing the interface and providing data.

A data-driven future?

At one of the early community group meetings there was a discussion about the legal and ethical implications of a service such as LAMP. The discussion turned to what might happen if students and researchers began questioning an institution's use of the data. At that point one member argued that the focus of discussion was changing, from one in which students are asking *about* the use of data, to one in which they are questioning why institutions are *not using* the data. What if a student failed her course and made a complaint that the university had not acted upon the data it held on her, to help prevent her from failing?

This is increasingly the reality for universities and colleges as students and researchers become accustomed to the personalized and data-driven experiences of the wider digital – and indeed physical library – environment. This, of course, means that academic institutions should not be complacent, and that of all the organizations that students will be interacting with, the university or college library will be one of the most trusted. There is a real opportunity for libraries both to take a strategic lead on campus in the data and analytics area and to use the data and their expertise to develop new services and improve the student experience.

But, as the discussions around data analysis make clear, LAMP is just one part of a wider analytics conversation. Across the academic sector there are considerations around data literacy, and for users of services like LAMP in particular. Importantly, LAMP will also enable libraries to consider analytics more broadly and to explore various approaches to gathering the data required for improving and developing services, from quantitative to qualitative approaches.

Chapter conclusion

This chapter has described two examples of developments in data and analytics that begin to move us away from thinking just about the services and systems we are building or procuring, to a realization that the real power lies in our ability to collect, share and interrogate the data at ever greater scales, and to undertake meaningful analysis that will lead to concrete action. LAMP demonstrates that we can, as communities and sectors, begin to share and collaborate on the technical infrastructure of analytics in order to ensure a focus on data quality, analysis and action at the local level. The work at the

Open University is helping to exemplify how a better understanding of the data locally, its flows and quality, can provide new functionality to existing systems and services and enable the library and the institution to think about what that data might also enable for its users.

The remaining chapters in this book concentrate on specific uses that the interaction, usage and other data captured by our institutions can yield – from demonstrating new forms of value and impact, through to opportunities arising from more qualitative types of data and analysis. In the next chapter we will explore the way that data and its analysis can inform the management of our collections.

Big and small data: further resources

If you'd like to find out more about the work described in this chapter, and access further reading and inspiration, below are additional resources for individuals and institutions interested in big and small data for libraries and for cultural heritage organizations more generally.

More on the case studies
- The RISE project at the Open University, www.open.ac.uk/blogs/RISE.
- Information on all aspects of LAMP can be found on the project blog, http://jisclamp.mimas.ac.uk.

Additional resources
- Jisc, Activity Data Programme, www.jisc.ac.uk/whatwedo/programmes/inf11/activitydata.aspx.
- Small data on Wikipedia, http://en.wikipedia.org/wiki/Small_data.

References

British Library (2014) The British Library Big Data Experiment, http://britishlibrary.typepad.co.uk/digital-scholarship/2014/06/the-british-library-big-data-experiment.html.

Dempsey, L. (2012) Big Data … Big Trend, http://orweblog.oclc.org/archives/002196.html.

Jisc (2012) Activity Data: delivering benefits from the data deluge, www.jisc.ac.uk/publications/reports/2012/activity-data-delivering-benefits. aspx#casestudies.

Pollock, R. (2013) What Do We Mean by Small Data?, http://blog.okfn.org/2013/04/26/what-do-we-mean-by-small-data.

Case Study 1.1

Brophy, J. and Bawden, D. (2005) Is Google Enough? Comparison of an internet search engine with academic library resources, *Aslib Proceedings*, **57** (6), 498–512.

Information Commissioner's Office, *Retaining Personal Data (Principle 5)*, www.ico.org.uk/for_organisations/data_protection/the_guide/information_standards/principle_5.

Knott, M. L., Bradley, D. R., DeGeorge, D. S. and Ottaviani, J. (2007) Catalog Information and User Expectations in an Amazoogle World: too much? Too little? *Against the Grain*, **19** (5), article 10, http://docs.lib.purdue.edu/atg/vol19/iss5/10.

Pattern, D. (2009) 'I Know What You Borrowed Last Summer': exploiting usage data in an academic library. Presentation at Internet Librarian International conference, www.slideshare.net/daveyp/ili2009-exploiting-usage-data.

Sero Consulting (2010) The JISC MOSAIC Project: making our scholarly activity information count, http://sero.co.uk/mosaic/100322_MOSAIC_Final_Report_v7_FINAL.pdf.

Siemens, G. (2013) Learning Analytics: the emergence of a discipline, *American Behavioral Scientist*, **57** (10), 1380–400.

Case Study 1.2

Stone, G. and Ramsden, B. (2013) Library Impact Data Project: looking for the link between library usage and student attainment, *College and Research Libraries*, **74** (6), 546–59.

Data-driven collections management

Chapter overview

Data-driven collections management is not a new concept for libraries. From reading lists to user recommendations, through to library management systems and the careful analysis of data in spreadsheets and other systems, using data to inform collections management and policy is a key part of curating a library collection. It is therefore of little surprise that libraries and librarians have, over the past few years, become increasingly interested in exploring more sophisticated and joined-up ways of taking advantage of library transaction and management data to help drive more informed and open approaches to decision making on collection management.

This chapter explores some of the most recent and innovative examples of how libraries are refining their collection-management processes by creating tools and applications that can utilize data to make more informed decisions about a wide range of collection-management decisions. Case Study 2.1, from Harvard University Library, explores the creation of a library analytics toolkit and dashboard with a primary focus on collection data. Here the data and visualizations are aimed both at supporting the librarians in their everyday decision making and at enabling users to see how collections have changed over time. Case Study 2.2 describes the work of the Copac Collections Management (CCM) tool and the development of a prototype shared collections management service for UK academic libraries – a service that will enable both local holdings analysis and comparison across other Copac research and specialist libraries in the UK:

- CASE STUDY 2.1 Dulin, K. and Spina, C., *Building an analytics toolkit at the Harvard Library* (Harvard University), p. 28
- CASE STUDY 2.2 Cousins, S. and Massam, D., *Collection management analytics: the Copac Collection Management tools project* (Mimas, University of Manchester), p. 35

The collections turn

Libraries increasingly find themselves in a double bind. While budgets are reduced or remain static, user demand for access to the library, its services and content continues to grow. Further compounding this situation are the changing expectations and demands on space from users, meaning that large physical collections need to be rethought and space has to be reconfigured to meet the changing demands of users.

At the same time, e-books and digital monographs present libraries with their own challenges. In the public sector especially, the delivery of e-books continues to be problematic, as the technical and legal issues blight the user experience and compromise the library's ability to deliver them to users (see the UK government's independent review of e-lending in England's public libraries for an insight into these issues – Sieghart, 2013). And, while students and researchers have largely embraced digital access to journal articles, the same is not true for the scholarly monograph. Research suggests (Jisc, RLUK and Ithaka, 2012) that academics require the hard-copy text for long-form reading and in-depth research, especially within the humanities, social sciences and mathematics.

For a long time in academic libraries it has been journals that have dominated discussion of academic print resources, while the book (or monograph) has been a somewhat neglected part of the collections management debate. This inattention is giving way to a sustained focus by libraries, researchers, funders and systems vendors, as there is an increasing realization that library print collections must be carefully and skilfully managed, space must be re-engineered for more social and collaborative uses and physical books must increasingly be seen as part of a larger collection, whether institutional/organizational, regional or even national.

There are the beginnings of a collections turn.

The collection challenges that libraries face, those technological, behavioural and economic examples described above, are the core drivers of this collections turn. Such a turn is defined by its use of data to provide insight into the entirety of the physical and digital collection as well as the space and the changing demands and expectations of users; it is a turn that emphasizes the whole collection. It also utilizes data to extend the overview beyond the local confines of the library and encompass an understanding of holdings elsewhere and of how the collective intelligence can help to inform local collection-management decisions. It is a repositioning of the local in the context of a national, distributed collection.

Managing the local collection

The collections turn that we are beginning to describe begins and ends with the local collection. Libraries must ensure that their collections continue to provide users with access to relevant resources and to respond to changing demands. The collections turn is primarily a recognition that collections are not built to be great collections in themselves but are there to serve their users – to connect them with the content they need.

Libraries are responding by introducing a number of innovative approaches to local collections management that are reducing the 'friction' between the user and the collection, in terms of both more 'formal' collections management and acquisition approaches and more playful or 'informal' approaches to collections data.

Patron-driven acquisition

Patron-driven acquisition (PDA) is an acquisitions approach which is driven by the user. Rather than the library purchasing materials on the user's behalf, and with a 'just in case' approach, PDA enables the user to trigger the purchase of material through the action of clicking on a catalogue link or similar. This 'just in time' approach has a number of distinct advantages for the library (for links to further research on the advantages of PDA see Stone et al., 2012):

1 *Cost effectiveness*: Only books or material that users actually want to access are purchased. In theory, the library isn't purchasing anything until a user clicks on a link to a book that they want to read.
2 *Increased usage and circulation*: Not only is it the case that the material is purchased at the point of need (ensuring that the content is used at least once), but it also tends to be that PDA material has a higher circulation in general. What one user thinks is worth reading tends to agree with what others think is worth reading too.
3 *Collection balance*: Despite the fears, research suggests that PDA and other forms of user-driven acquisition help the development of a balanced collection

(Shen et al., 2011).

These shifting modes of acquisition are still relatively new developments. There are questions about the costs associated with these approaches, but fundamentally they demonstrate the way in which libraries are removing the barriers between the collection and its items and the user. Approaches like PDA enable users to directly affect the collections they use. But the circulation and management data used by libraries to make collections-management decisions, can also have a role in more playful approaches to engaging users with the collections.

Gamifying collections

The ubiquity of mobile devices means that we are comfortable – indeed we expect to be able – to interact between our physical presence and location and online applications and games. Additional layers are progressively being added to our actions and activities, with the aim of improving our experience of and engagement in those activities.

Gamification 'involves applying game design thinking to non-game applications to make them more fun and engaging' (http://gamification.org). While this is still a very new way to engage library users, a number of projects and companies are beginning to explore the potential for gamifying the library experience.

One of the best known in the UK is Library Game (http://librarygame. co.uk). Library Game uses library systems data – not necessarily the kind of data we might associate with an innovative, user-centred game – to collect participating users' activity and transaction data. As a Library Game player borrows or returns a book that data is used by the game to provide a social element to the circulation process, showing what other users are borrowing, etc., as well as awarding points for different activities and moving the user up (or down) the scoreboard. Users can also leave reviews of books, create friends' lists and see their borrowing history. Importantly, Library Game also provides that data back to the library so that it is able to analyse behaviours and borrowing patterns to inform both its services and collections, utilizing a depth of data not previously available.

Libraries are also utilizing existing applications and services, such as SCVNGR (www.scvngr.com), as a way to encourage students and users to undertake tasks within the library; specifically they are using them for library inductions.

It would be easy to dismiss such approaches as superficial and a passing fad. Yet this is increasingly how we interact with our environment, and these kinds of experiences are still at an early stage of development – they are only going to get better! Critically, they also point to a new way of engaging our users with the collections and services that libraries manage. This engagement is both about making the experience more fun and about using that engagement to generate intelligence and data that can be fed back to the services and collections to continually improve them. These approaches create a positive feedback loop where gradually more in-depth and richer data is generated that is used to further improve and refine services and collections.

These new and emerging approaches to local collections development, strategy and management become even more critical as the data begins to inform collections-management decision making beyond the local institution and library, at a sector, regional and even national level.

Managing the 'national' collection

As we have seen, a number of interesting developments are taking place in libraries to help transform local collections management and strategies. And, as library and collections data becomes more accessible, better curated, timelier and more accurate it begins to open up possibilities beyond the local library and enables decisions to be made on a regional or national level. This regional or national organization of collections describes the second part of the collections turn: the local collection is situated within and contributes to a broader regional, sector or national collection (or collections).

As Lorcan Dempsey et al. argue: 'One important trend is that libraries and the organizations that provide services to them will devote more attention to system-wide organization of collections – whether the "system" is a consortium, a region or a country' (Dempsey et al., 2013). This focus on the system-wide level is already becoming well established in the UK and elsewhere. The UK Research Reserve (UKRR) is an exemplar of the development of a national and collaborative approach to the challenge of retaining low-use print journals. The collaboration between academic libraries and the British Library enables its members to de-duplicate print journal holdings if the same title is held by three other UKRR members (including a copy in the British Library), ensuring long-term access to journal titles while allowing libraries to free up precious space and resources. In particular, UKRR has been successful in building a fabric of trust between participants. Mechanisms such as formal agreements and the inclusion of the British Library's Document Supply Service have been key in developing trust. Reliable, comprehensive and timely data has helped libraries to be confident in basing local decisions on what is happening elsewhere nationally.

In the US the Maine Shared Collections Strategy (MSCS) is a collaboration between nine partner institutions working to broaden collection access across the state of Maine. MSCS is interesting for a number of reasons. Firstly, the strategy is aiming to focus on access to collections, preservation and resource sharing; it is not explicitly about disposal or de-duplication of materials in the same way that UKRR is. Secondly, the strategy also includes books, which until recently have largely been excluded from national or regional approaches to collections management. MSCS is beginning to address some of the challenges that the monograph presents to shared collections strategies, including being able to offer 'print on demand' services in relation to the millions of digital books available within the Hathi Trust collection. This approach may provide a way of exploiting digital copies while serving an ongoing preference for print, expressed by both researchers and students (Kay, Stephens and DeNoyer, 2014).

This increasing interest in the challenges that the transition from print to digital monographs presents to libraries and institutions is something that is being explored as part of the National Monograph Strategy (NMS) in the UK. The project is exploring the potential for a national approach to the creation, collection, preservation and digitization of scholarly monographs. The project has outlined eight high-level ideas to address some of the challenges presented by the scholarly monograph, including a national monograph knowledge base, which would provide a comprehensive and open bibliographic and holdings database enabling the development of new applications and services for libraries, systems vendors, publishers and users. Much of what will underpin a national strategy for monographs in the UK will be based on accurate and timely data that can help to inform and drive decision making, both locally and system-wide. Further information on the NMS ideas and the strategy itself can be found on the project's webpage: www.jisc.ac.uk/research/projects/national-monograph-strategy.

These examples of regional and national collection management each provide exemplars of how data is being used to help drive decision making at that system-wide level. This picture maps onto the two case studies below, which describe the innovative use of data locally to drive collections-management decisions and improve the user experience, and how local data can be aggregated to provide institutions with a national picture, helping inform local decisions in the context of a national collections landscape.

The two case studies also make it clear, however, that the data on its own is not sufficient. The data, intelligence and systems that underpin these services and strategies are tools that enable librarians to ask new questions – but do not necessarily provide easy answers. They enable libraries to explore new opportunities and librarians to develop their skills and knowledge so as to curate and manage collections that meet their users' needs, as well as manage to balance the economic and technological changes that are also driving change.

Data-driven collections management can be transformative, as these case studies begin to describe, but it can achieve this only when the right skills and expertise are on the ground to ensure that data-driven insights can be turned into concrete actions.

CASE STUDY 2.1

Building an analytics toolkit at the Harvard Library

Kim Dulin (Harvard Library Innovation Lab) and Carli Spina (Harvard Library)

Introduction

In these days of data-driven decision making, libraries are starting to look for ways to use the data that they already collect to better serve their users while maximizing their budget's reach. At the Harvard Library Innovation Lab (http://librarylab.law.harvard.edu), part of the Harvard Law School Library, these two goals served as the jumping-off point for developing Haystacks, a library analytics toolkit. Haystacks visualizes library data in order to help provide insights into library activities, better inform library users and enable library staff to make smarter decisions in their day-to-day work. Over the last three years the Haystacks development team has conducted extensive research into data-collection practices used at Harvard University Libraries: the resulting tool is designed to search through and visualize collection data for over 12 million items in the Harvard Library's collection. This case study describes the process we followed in creating the tool and offers some lessons learned for others who may be considering similar projects.

Background research and project preparation

The original inspiration for the analytics tool came from an earlier project called Checkout the Checkouts. Checkout the Checkouts generated a web page with information on the most frequently circulated items in the Harvard Library collection. Results could be further subdivided by the user's school affiliation (i.e. Law School, Divinity School, Graduate School of Design, etc.). While this provided a nice snapshot of a specific type of library data, the team quickly realized that the tool would be much more powerful if it could incorporate other library data into a format that was similarly easy to navigate.

This idea grew into a proposal to build a library analytics toolkit. The proposal was submitted to the Harvard Library Lab, an on-campus organization that awards grants from the Arcadia Fund (www.arcadiafund. org.uk/) to support projects that 'create better services for Harvard students and faculty and play a leading role in shaping the information society of the future' (Harvard Library Lab Program Description and Guidelines, 2012). The initial proposal envisioned an open-source software package that would allow libraries to track and visualize various types of data, such as electronic resource usage and reference transaction statistics. The Library administration was particularly interested in a tool that would help it to track how resource expenditures translated to use.

The proposal was accepted and initial funding was granted, with the understanding that the first stage of the project would involve extensive interviews with staff across the Harvard Libraries to determine how statistics were collected and what information would be most useful. This stage would ensure that the product developed would integrate well with how that data was already being collected and used. The team collected information about how data regarding library space utilization, reference interactions, acquisitions, circulation and electronic resource usage was gathered. This research revealed that various campus libraries and even different departments within the same library collected data in different ways. These differences often related to the varying types of services offered across the campus and the unique purposes for which each department collected data. We also found that acquisitions and collection data from various publishers often differed in format and availability, particularly for electronic resources. While the Counting Online Usage of Networked Electronic Resources (COUNTER) standards have helped to make recent usage information more compatible across electronic resources, we still found this data difficult to integrate with other collection and usage information, particularly for time periods prior to the advent of the COUNTER standards.

During the interview phase we looked beyond Harvard at how other libraries, archives, museums and similar institutions were collecting, using and sharing their own data. The work of other institutions influenced some of our early ideas about how the toolkit might be used. We looked at several existing web dashboards that appealed to us and seemed to match our needs, including North Carolina State University Library's Dataviews Dashboard (now known as By the Numbers, www.lib.ncsu.edu/bythenumbers), the Indianapolis Museum of Art's Dashboard (http://dashboard.imamuseum.org) and one then in development at the Brown University Library. These projects helped us to determine how data might be visualized so that it would be both useful for library staff and informative for library users. With this information, we focused on designing the toolkit as a dashboard.

This research stage culminated in a report (Spina, 2011) that laid out the goals for the project and identified which types of data might best integrate into the initial iteration of the toolkit. This document advised that the toolkit should take advantage of the data already available at the Harvard Libraries and that the design should be extensible so as to encompass additional data in later iterations. With this in mind, we focused initially on visualizing collection data, so that collection development librarians could immediately use the tool and so that library users could have a window into how the use of Harvard Library's collections has changed over time.

Choosing a developer

From the beginning we knew that we wanted a tool to visualize multiple types of library data in a useful and somewhat unusual format. We did not intend the tool to be used only by librarians; rather, we wanted it to be useful to general library users interested in discovering not only what items were collected by the Harvard Library but also how they were used. This objective dovetailed with the Library Innovation Lab's focus on user metrics (see for example: StackLife, http://stacklife.harvard.edu/; Library Cloud, http://librarycloud.harvard.edu/; and Checkout the Checkouts, http://librarylab.law.harvard.edu/checkout/).

We aimed for the dashboard design to display relevant metrics in a modular format and respond to user input. After reviewing the dashboard format and thinking about our users' needs, we decided that we wanted to allow our users to dig more deeply into the data and manipulate it in ways that the sample dashboards did not allow. Based on our knowledge of advancements in data visualization, these features seemed possible.

To achieve this advanced data visualization, we decided that we needed to hire an outside specialist. We interviewed local data visualization companies, and found Rosten Woo, who had previously worked with our designer, to be the best fit (www.wehavenoart.net). Woo had never worked with library data but he was intrigued by the project and was interested in libraries in general. Once Woo had been briefed on the project he engaged the services of two colleagues, Sha Hwang and Rachel Binx, both data visualization specialists (http://postarchitectural.com, http://rachelbinx.com).

To help the developers understand the needs of the library community, Harvard librarians crafted use cases from which the developers could design the first iteration of the toolkit. Our primary use case featured a collection development librarian interested in seeing how the library's collection had developed over time. Other use cases included a librarian interested in developing a research guide on a particular topic, a library administrator planning a weeding project based on circulation data and a library user interested in tracing the history of research on a topic by seeing when books were published. These use cases provided the foundation for development decisions and proved particularly useful in targeting future revisions.

We collaborated with the developers mainly via telephone or Skype meetings every few weeks. Over time the tool was modified extensively, and the final version appeared strikingly different than previous ones. Figure 2.1 below shows a very early version with modular components that look somewhat like a dashboard. Ultimately, we decided that this version did not synthesize and display data in the manner that we were hoping for, but it was useful to demonstrate the concept and to show how the available data could be manipulated.

The next version of the toolkit, shown in Figure 2.2, completely revised the way that the data was presented to make it easier to dive deeper into the information. Users were able to search by date and view the data retrieved in a graphical format. They could begin their search from within the Library of Congress Subject Heading (LCSH) hierarchy embedded in the tool. Search results could be instantly manipulated by clicking on the graphical interface. The current iteration, shown in Figure 2.3, looks entirely different from

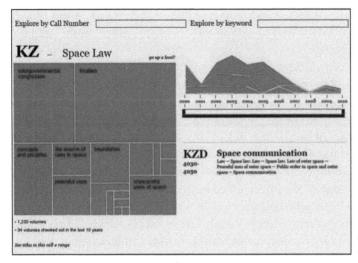

Figure 2.1
Initial wireframes for dashboard

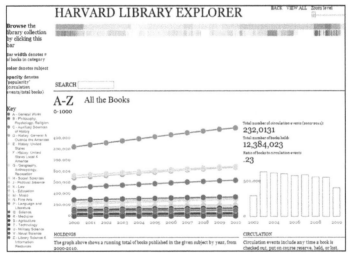

Figure 2.2
Modified Harvard library explorer dashboard

previous ones. It reflects a wholesale revision based on information from the use cases and the additional data points, plus significant modifications in search and display. This version switched the visualization style to a bubble format, pulled individual item data into the display and deployed new navigational features as well as the ability to select and export data.

Technical challenges

The Innovation Lab staff and Woo's team shared the work on the toolkit. We received supplemental funding from the Harvard Library Lab to add features after the first version was launched.

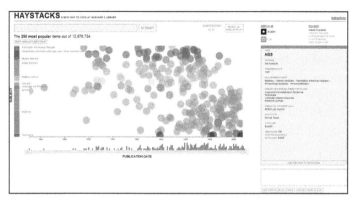

Figure 2.3
*'Bubble'
visualization
wireframe for the
Harvard library
explorer
dashboard*

Library Innovation Lab in-house developer, Paul Deschner, did the back-end data-wrangling work and developed the API that allowed the data visualization experts to pull in Harvard data. Deschner's work required him to gather data in three areas: e-download statistics, hierarchically structured Library of Congress (LOC) classification data, and LOC call-number supplementation for non-LOC-classed items. E-download statistics presented the greatest challenges, and automated solutions had to be developed so as to handle large amounts of source data; the data, in turn, was at times loosely structured and spread across ad hoc collected files with many different formats and data structures. The LOC classification data, which was bureaucratically difficult to obtain from LOC, needed to be restructured along hierarchical lines, and corrupt source data had to be fixed. LOC call-number supplementation required designing routines to match LCSH profiles and assign call numbers to items without them. Despite these challenges, Deschner described the work as rewarding, since all three solutions resulted in major new additions to our open data platform, which allowed easy access for developers who might want to build on the application in the future.

New challenges arose once the data was fed to Woo and his team. The massive data set needed to be scaled to an individual level that made sense for the use cases. There were many individual items to track (over 12 million objects, each with 10–30 fields) and the data was most interesting when the user was able to view it at the item level (e.g. it is probably more interesting to get the titles of books about 'cacti' than to know how many books about 'cacti' there are). In Woo's previous work, it was not essential to drill down to such a granular level. Woo explained, 'If you were doing population statistics, it's enough to know a few general things about 12 million people (race, income, etc.) but here it's as if we want to be able to drill down to know each of those 12 million people's first name.'

A second challenge involved the peculiar nature of the LCSH, which are arranged in a somewhat outdated taxonomical structure. Woo noted that it was quite a bit of work to make sense of this giant, sprawling, semi-proprietary taxonomy. The developers wanted to be faithful to the spirit of the actual library, in which 'each item gets one location', but also wanted to provide the flexibility that web users are used to, such as mixing and matching search terms of their own choosing.

Woo also found that the unique nature of library materials presented a steeper learning curve than he had faced in other projects. In every project a developer needs to understand the data and to familiarize himself with the conventions and nuances of a particular dataset. Library datasets have a large range of differences, and different disciplines use the materials in different ways. Resources in one discipline may have checkouts several orders of magnitude larger than those in other disciplines, but that does not necessarily mean that they are that much more important.

Conclusions, next steps and recommendations

While the toolkit is now in a form that achieves many of our goals, it remains a work in progress. In its current format, we anticipate that it will give library staff a view of how the collection is being used that was not available with previously existing tools. It will also help collection development librarians to identify trends in both acquisitions and use that will make it easier to predict and meet user needs. While we have primarily focused on creating a tool for librarians, we also hope that the toolkit will be a useful discovery tool for library users. It offers a new window into our collection and makes it easy to navigate through the holdings on a subject in a visual way. It also offers the public greater insight than ever before into how the Harvard Library collection is used.

Despite this success, there are still areas for improvement. In creating the tool, we worked with various sorts of data, including MARC records, LOC class numbers and LCSH, and COUNTER statistics, but we had hoped to include additional data, such as financial information to show dollars spent versus usage. This ultimately proved to be unworkable because of Harvard's complex library structure and the desire to keep financial issues private. We ultimately determined that if we wanted to include this data in the future we could develop a spin-off version to be kept on a secure internal server.

We expect to launch Haystacks to the Harvard Library community in the next few months. Once it has been officially launched, we plan to collect feedback and conduct usability testing to determine whether it meets the needs of the various target audiences. This process will give us the information we need to continue to modify and add to the existing tool. The Harvard Library Lab, which funded the work on the toolkit, will also fund documentation, public distribution of code, future hosting and outreach. As with all of our projects, we will offer the code under an open source licence. We hope that other libraries will use our existing project as a starting place for their own data visualization projects, or will at least find inspiration in the way that we have combined our data to offer new insights into our collection.

CASE STUDY 2.2

Collection management analytics: the Copac Collection Management tools project

Shirley Cousins and Diana Massam (Mimas, University of Manchester)

The Copac Collection Management tools project (CCM tools) aims to deliver a collection management support service, providing tools that enable library staff to make more informed decisions around their collection-related activity, such as material disposal, conservation or digitization, collection assessment and development.

CCM tools is a Jisc-funded project which began in 2011 with a Research Libraries UK (RLUK, www.rluk.ac.uk) initiated collaboration between the White Rose Consortium libraries (the Universities of Leeds, Sheffield and York) and the Copac team at Mimas (www.mimas.ac.uk). We have worked closely with RLUK throughout and members of the RLUK community have played a key role, with most recently the libraries of the University of Manchester, the Royal College of Surgeons of England and Senate House Library, University of London, joining the project to take the work forward.

Copac brings together the catalogues of a growing range of UK and Irish research libraries, creating an increasingly valuable picture of library collections. We know from user surveys that some library staff make use of the service to assist their collection-management decision making; however, Copac is designed primarily as a public catalogue service, so it has limitations in this context. At Mimas we are enthusiastic about the potential for making the Copac data work harder, increasing the benefits to our contributing libraries and, more widely, to the library community. So, within the CCM tools project we have developed a new interface to the Copac data that provides library staff with a range of facilities to support exploration of the data at the collection level.

By enabling decisions to be made within the context of comparative analytics, the CCM tools support libraries wanting to benchmark specific collections within the wider national collection landscape and identify key areas of commonality or difference against other collections locally or nationally. The project has been driven by the collection management needs and the enthusiasm of the partner libraries; this has been a crucial element in the success of the project so far, grounding the technical development within the real requirements of library staff, with Mimas providing technical expertise to translate those requirements into practical reality. The initial interface-development activity was carried out alongside use-case development by the libraries, with ongoing iterative technical development as the partners worked on case studies. In this way the tools were formed to support the range of activities reflected in the early use cases, and honed through practical use.

The CCM tools pilot

The current CCM tools interface allows users to gain a valuable insight into the collections of our contributing libraries, with options for exploring collections broadly between institutions, or looking in detail at individual materials.

There are three search screens supporting:

- manual searching for small numbers of documents or individual items
- batch searching for large numbers of documents, e.g. for reviewing collections using a file of local record numbers exported from a library's local catalogue
- keyword searching for collections in particular subject areas, by specific authors, etc.

Searches can include library or geographic limits, for example a limit to a particular region can improve understanding of a collection within the local context. Searches can also be tailored to show items held by a specified number of libraries, for example, to show just the commonly held items to assist making withdrawal decisions. It is also possible to apply varying degrees of results de-duplication in situations where the caution shown in the creation of Copac-consolidated records is not required.

Search results can be viewed as Copac records, but the main focus of the results display is the data visualization and the export options. Records loaded into Copac are de-duplicated, with matching records being formed into consolidated records that represent (as far as possible) all our contributors' holdings of a particular document. This means that the Copac records contain valuable information about the number of libraries holding a copy of each document in the database. This holdings data underpins the data visualizations that allow the searcher to assess their own holdings within the search results in relation to those of other contributors. Figure 2.4 illustrates

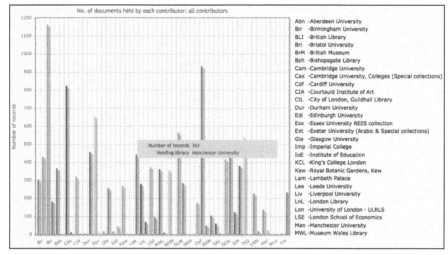

Figure 2.4 *CCM tools results visualization: the graphical presentation of a result set showing the number of documents held by each contributor within the search results*

the results of a search, expressed as a graph that shows the number of documents within the result set that are held by each contributor. The search results can also be exported in different forms for further local analysis.

In 2013 we released a beta version of the CCM tools to a wider audience comprising the RLUK member libraries, all of whom contribute their catalogues to Copac. This is allowing for testing by a much wider community and providing valuable feedback on the current functionality, as well as looking at new use cases within these libraries. Alongside this we are developing support materials and making provision for community support mechanisms.

The project is still in a pilot phase, but has been very well received, to the extent that some of the participating libraries are already beginning to use the CCM tools as part of their business-as-usual activity. Some of the range of activity being explored can be illustrated in the case studies our partner libraries have been undertaking.

Case studies

We have collected a range of case study reports from users which demonstrate how the CCM tools can deliver added value and efficiency across a broad range of collection-management activities. These case studies are available on the CCM Blog and also via the CCM User Forum (http://copac.ac.uk/innovations/collections-management). Outputs from the tools enable library staff to take an analytical approach to making collection-management decisions which also have wider implications across a range of library processes and policy areas.

Participating libraries have used the tools in a variety of contexts to facilitate stock withdrawal, collection profiling and conservation or digitization work. The added value of the analytics that the tools provide has been demonstrated in many ways.

Stock management

Supporting decisions about stock withdrawal within the context of increasing pressure on space is a key benefit of the CCM tools. Despite the increasing availability and adoption of electronic materials, most libraries are under significant space pressure, in part due to the continuing acquisition of print monographs, but also through the need to support newly developing forms of teaching and research within the library. So this fairly clear-cut task is often the first area of experimentation for libraries embarking on their own use of the tools, providing clear statistical evidence and time-saving benefits.

By allowing libraries to check their own stock against the holdings of other libraries, and identify those titles which are rare or unique nationally, the tools provide a benchmark against which stock withdrawal or weeding decisions can be made, often in conjunction with data from other sources, such as usage statistics. Stock management tends to be a key driver in encouraging participants to try out the tools and we have reports of projects ranging in size from a brief assessment of 84 items in a library store to a major project resulting in the withdrawal of over 2,500 low-use monographs.

A good example of this activity is the work done at Sheffield (Ward, 2013) to withdraw low-use monographs from a document store so as to provide space for materials being relegated from elsewhere in the library. Sheffield was concerned that document withdrawal, necessary for local reasons, should not result in the loss of materials not widely held elsewhere. Based on local withdrawal criteria, a workflow was developed that used a list of ISBNs generated via the library management system to batch search CCM tools. From the results, a minimum cut-off of eight holding libraries was defined to permit withdrawal of an item. The data exported from CCM tools was then re-imported into Sheffield's library management system to generate a pick-list for withdrawal of items from the shelves. This allowed 29 metres of shelving to be freed up, but with the assurance of retaining items that are less widely held.

The Sheffield work also illustrates how, by using the tools, libraries have been able to design far more automated workflows for stock-withdrawal activities than would otherwise have been possible. In other cases libraries report that they had previously performed manual stock checks on Copac when initiating stock weeds. This time-consuming task can be eliminated when it is replaced with a batch item search using the CCM tools. Significant savings in staff time are identified in many of our case studies which can be quantified as direct cost savings to institutions. For example, staff at the University of Manchester established a workflow using the CCM tools to identify and process stock for withdrawal which took staff four to five days to complete. The team calculated that manually checking the same stock prior to withdrawal would have taken the same staff seven weeks to complete (Copac, 2012a).

The use of comparative statistical data to support stock retention decisions also enables managers to demonstrate clearly the rationale for decision making. This has had a positive impact on the level of support for such potentially controversial activity from users and academics, who can be reassured about continuing access at a local or national level. Not only do the graph and map visualizations help to clarify collection-related issues for stakeholders, but they also help the library staff involved to present a much more 'professional' case for the decisions they are taking.

We also have examples of libraries using the tools to support decisions regarding conservation and digitization, taking into account the rarity of individual items. The tools enable staff effort to be targeted on items which are identified as having maximum benefit to the collection, and therefore increase efficiency in this time-consuming area.

However, while facilitating decision making, the provision of data about other library holdings also flagged up the need for libraries to address their existing policies on stock retention and preservation. Decisions need to be made about the threshold for considering an item to be rare or unique, i.e. how many copies of an item held elsewhere make it a rare item? Even when they are identified as rare or unique, what are the policies for retaining such items? There are differences in approach even among the examples we have collected, including where regional policies may exist. These decisions also have a national dimension when considering the broader concept of the development of national monograph collection policies.

Collection profiling

Going beyond support for stock management activity outlined above, the participating libraries have also been keen to exploit the potential of the CCM tools in collection profiling and benchmarking. Various case studies have demonstrated the value of the tools in enabling libraries to deepen their understanding of their collections both individually and in relation to other libraries.

We have had reports posted to the CCM Forum describing activity around the profiling of specific subject areas, confirming areas of collection strength, discovering previously hidden areas of significance, enhancing special collections and identifying heritage collections. All these case studies reflect the tools' unique functionality in providing direct comparisons to other collections in an easy-to-use format.

In an environment within which institutions increasingly have access to the same electronic resources, many universities are recognizing that areas of their print collections are prime assets to be conserved and promoted as unique resources, enhancing the reputation of the institution. The CCM tools can help libraries to identify those areas of their collections which have regional or national significance, providing opportunities for marketing the library, as well as supporting applications for funding to conserve or develop materials in those areas. Previously, recognition might have come about through collecting expert knowledge and opinion from library and academic staff: a necessarily subjective approach, and one that entails the danger of losing knowledge as specialist staff move or retire. The use of comparative data from the tools enables what one library has described as 'a sounder and evidence-based approach' to collection analysis (Emly, Horne and Pindar, 2012).

The ability to collect clear statistical evidence is frequently cited as a key benefit in collection-profiling work. Such evidence can be used to confirm previously anecdotal or instinctive 'hunches' about a library's collection strengths. For example, the University of St Andrews reported that:

> The visual representation of the data, both the graphs and map, are instantly illuminating and supported our theory.
>
> (Helen Faulds, Deputy Collections Manager, University of St Andrews Library)

Combining data to best effect

As familiarity with the tools has increased, so has the complexity of the projects which some participants have completed. A common feature of these projects is the additional value to be obtained by combining library analytics data from a range of sources with contextual collection data. This encompasses how the collection fits within the national context, as well as against specific competing or high-profile institutions, producing a detailed profile of a subject area within the library.

This approach is exemplified by work done at the University of York (Elder, 2013) on building up a detailed collection profile in one specific area by bringing together a variety of statistics from different sources; these related to features of the collection such as usage, age profile, stock acquisition rate), etc. York performed a gap analysis, identifying stock held in common by the top-listed non-copyright libraries, which are therefore shown to have the strongest collections in a specific subject area. This information was subsequently used to produce a list of titles for potential purchase to strengthen the coverage for a newly developing subject area at the University of York (Figure 2.5).

The initial collection profile report was very well received, being seen as a valuable tool for working with academic departments in developing collections within their subject and generating interest from other subject liaison staff wanting to do similar work in their own area. This activity is now embedded as part of the York '5 Year Content Strategy' and the reports are encouraging and facilitating discussions between the library and academic departments in regard to evaluating stock selection and use, thus contributing to more positive collaborative relationships.

Other potential uses for complex collection profiles include providing support for funding bids or identifying collaborators for joint venture, as suggested by participants using the tools in increasingly creative ways.

Going forward

As the participants have gained familiarity with the tools and the CCM tools project has progressed, they have been finding new ways to explore the collections and developing new use cases as they gain a sense of what is possible. This has not only provided concrete information about collections, but has enabled the participants to carry out trial collection research in areas that were previously too costly, or simply not possible. This increasing understanding of the tools' potential has also broadened the focus of interest

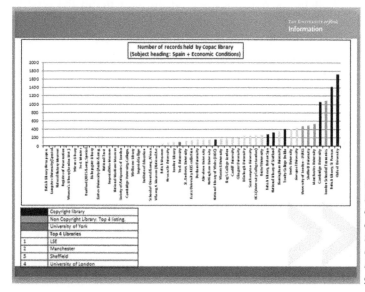

Figure 2.5
Extract from York collection profile: data exported from CCM tools used to generate locally tailored graphs

from relatively clear-cut issues, such as withdrawals, into diverse areas: from improved stakeholder relationships, through library marketing, to identifying potential collaborators in collection-development activity or grant applications.

To take the CCM tools into full service, further work is needed in a number of areas. Technical development is ongoing; the collection analytics are dependent on the quality of the record consolidation within Copac, which in turn is dependent on the underlying record quality. At the time of writing we are developing a new Copac database with, among other things, enhanced record de-duplication; but this will never be perfect and it is important to understand the limitations of the data. However, the match process errs on the side of caution, and so it will tend to over-emphasize rarity, which is reassuring in terms of withdrawal decisions, while the CCM tools de-duplication facilities provide users with control over the degree of de-duplication desired for a particular search.

Alongside this, another future activity is the gathering of further evidence for a business case as we work towards moving from a pilot project towards a full service. An important next step is to explore use cases and requirements for the wider library community, including libraries that are not contributors to Copac. We have had interest from a range of different libraries outside the pilot group and we need to look at how we might best support this broader community. Many of the existing facilities will work for any library, for example the ISBN batch search or the export of data for local evaluation; however, we will be working with non-contributing libraries to ensure that we understand their requirements fully and provide them with the most effective support.

Even at this early stage users can see significant benefits in the type of collection data the tools can supply. In our recent survey of trial users (the results are available on the CCM tools blog http://copac.ac.uk/innovations/collections-management) there were comments across areas such as 'speed', 'benchmarking', and support for withdrawals. Other comments related to the importance of having concrete data to go beyond the 'anecdotal' understanding, in particular for working with other stakeholders. One user valued

> Increasing the amount of data and knowledge about the library collection that I can report on to senior management.

Another commented that

> Understanding the profile of our collections in comparison to other UK collections has been politically helpful.

The CCM tools will not provide 'the answer' to everyone's collection-management questions, but this type of data can provide valuable supporting information. And, as the York case study illustrates, collection analytics can be used effectively alongside data from a range of other sources to provide a compelling case, which could be adapted in many different situations.

Alongside the development of practical collection-management support tools, there has been a second thread running throughout the CCM project. This has involved a dialogue with the community exploring shared approaches to collection-management activity. The CCM tools initially grew out of a concern for the managed withdrawal of materials as libraries seek to free up space. In many research libraries checking for 'last copies' is an integral but time-consuming part of the stock-editing process. The CCM tools can assist with the practicalities of the process, in terms of the speed and ease of gathering data for informed decision making. However, the provision of fast and easy access to new collection analytics places into sharp relief the need to carry out this collection-management activity within a broader context.

Within the research libraries, the issue of stock withdrawal raises important questions about the extent to which libraries should consider the needs of the wider research community beyond the individual institution. There is a growing sense of the importance of this wider context and the need to ensure that the broader regional and national document collection is not diminished by local decisions about collection disposal. That which is redundant in one library may prove to be rare and valuable more widely. This is an issue that the project has explored through community consultation, where there was an emerging consensus over the need for collaboration to ensure that researchers continue to have access to the full range of materials through a distributed National Research Collection of Monographs (Copac, 2012b). More recently, project members have been involved in the Jisc National Monographs Strategy project and the development of the project's strategy roadmap (Showers, 2014) exploring problem areas across the monograph landscape. In the long term we hope that Copac and the CCM tools can offer valuable collection analytics to facilitate local collection-management activity across a range of areas, as well as being a focus for a regional and national approach to sustainable collection management, supporting collaboration between institutions and sharing of materials, protecting the UK research collection into the future.

Acknowledgements

A major factor in our success so far has been a highly engaged, supportive and effective Project Board. We are indebted to Mike Mertens from RLUK; Brian Clifford and Michael Emly from the University of Leeds; Gary Ward from the University of Sheffield; Ruth Elder from the University of York;

Christine Wise from Senate House Library; Sandra Bracegirdle from the University of Manchester; Thalia Knight from the Royal College of Surgeons, England; and Ben Showers from Jisc.

Chapter conclusion

This chapter has described the ways in which data is helping to inform decision making by libraries both locally (which, in the case of Harvard, is a multi-library institution) and within a region, sector or nation, as in the case of the CCM tools. What both case studies describe is the increasing convergence of these two types of activity: increasingly, the decisions that libraries make at a local level will inform and be informed by those events and decisions happening across libraries at a sectoral and national level. Any distinction between the local library's data and that of the consortium, region or sector will erode. While this will inevitably present libraries and institutions with challenges – as innovations such as patron-driven acquisition have done – it will also provide libraries and the users they serve with exciting new opportunities. The idea of a national collection becomes a very real possibility.

However, we must be careful not to become too complacent in the 'collections turn' we are describing here. While analytics provides us with a clear picture of what people have done (i.e. borrowed a particular book), it doesn't provide us with any data on how they did it or what the experience was like. If libraries and cultural heritage institutions really want to begin transforming their services, and the experience of their users, new forms of data and insight will need to be explored. This exploration of new types of insight will be examined in our next chapter, on demonstrating the impact and value of the library through analytics.

Data-driven collections management: further resources

If you'd like to find out more about the work described in this chapter, and access further reading and inspiration, below are additional resources for individuals and institutions interested in how data and new data-driven approaches can inform collections management and development.

National/regional shared collections strategies and services

* The National Monograph Strategy includes a literature/landscape review that covers a lot of relevant material around collections management and national/international activity in this space, http://monographs.jiscinvolve.org/wp/2013/07/31/monographs-landscape-report/.

- More information on the Maine Shared Collections Strategy (MSCS) can be found at its website, www.maineinfonet.org/mscs.
- More information on the UK Research Reserve (UKRR) can be found at its website, www.ukrr.ac.uk.
- The Hathi Trust, www.hathitrust.org.

Library game examples
- Library Game, http://librarygame.co.uk
- ALA Game Making Interest Group Wiki, http://gamemakinginterestgroup.wikispaces.com/Library+Game+Examples.
- Rice, Scott, Library Guides at Appalachian State University, http://guides.library.appstate.edu/content.php?pid=449216&sid=3680579.

References

Dempsey, L., Lavoie, B., Malpas, C., Connaway, L. S., Schonfeld, R. C., Shipengrover, J. D. and Waibel, G. (2013) *Understanding the Collective Collection: towards a system-wide perspective on library print collections*, OCLC Research, www.oclc.org/research/publications/library/2013/2013-09.pdf.

Jisc, RLUK and Ithaka (2012) *UK Survey of Academics 2012*, www.sr.ithaka.org/research-publications/ithaka-sr-jisc-rluk-uk-survey-academics-2012.

Kay, D., Stephens, O. and DeNoyer, A. (2014) *Last Copy Services: what are the opportunities and benefits of collaboration?* www.iii.com/sites/default/files/imce/UKInnovative%20Conversation2014-05_Last%20Copy.pdf.

Shen, L., Cassidy, E. D., Elmore, E., Griffin, G., Manolovitz, T., Martinez, M. and Turney, L. M. (2011) Headfirst into Patron-Driven Acquisition Pool: a comparison of librarian selections versus patron purchases, *Journal of Electronic Resources Librarianship*, **23**, 203–18.

Sieghart, W. (2013) *An Independent Review of E-Lending in Public Libraries in England*, https://www.gov.uk/government/publications/an-independent-review-of-e-lending-in-public-libraries-in-england.

Stone, G., Pattern, D., Devenney, A., Larkins, A., White, S., Earney, L. and Bascones, M. (2012) HIKE Project, https://library3.hud.ac.uk/blogs/hike/2012/12/06/patron-driven-acquisition.

Case Study 2.1

Harvard Library Lab Program Description and Guidelines (2012) https://osc.hul.harvard.edu/sites/default/files/LibraryLab_Guidelines_Dec2012.pdf.

Spina, C. (2011) *Recommendations for the Design of the Library Analytics Toolkit*, https://osc.hul.harvard.edu/sites/default/files/Analytics_Recommendations.pdf.

Case Study 2.2

Copac (2012a) *Case Studies Synthesis Report*,
    http://copac.ac.uk/innovations/collections-management/wp-content/uploads/
    2012/07/CaseStudiesSynthesis.pdf.
Copac (2012b) *CCM Tools Project, Retention and Preservation: final report*, July 2012,
    http://copac.ac.uk/innovations/collections-management/reports.
Elder, R. (2013) *Use of the CCM Tool for Gap Analysis at the University of York Library,
    Case Study 2: York University, CCM tools beta trial: introductory event*, London and
    Manchester, July 2013, http://copac.ac.uk/innovations/collections-
    management/2013/07/ccm-beta-trial-introductory-events.
Emly, M., Horne, J. and Pindar, M. (2012) *Leeds Case Study 1: large scale use of the
    Copac tool to profile collections*, July 2012,
    http://copac.ac.uk/innovations/collections-management/case-studies.
Showers, B. (2014) The Jisc *National Monographs Strategy* Roadmap,
    www.jisc.ac.uk/reports/a-national-monograph-strategy-roadmap.
Ward, G. (2013) *Stock Withdrawal Workflow, Case Study 1: Sheffield University, CCM
    Tools Beta Trial: introductory event*, London and Manchester, July 2013,
    http://copac.ac.uk/innovations/collections-management/2013/07/ccm-beta-trial-
    introductory-events.

Using data to demonstrate library impact and value

Chapter overview

Libraries, and cultural heritage institutions more generally, are increasingly being asked to demonstrate their value and impact. This chapter aims to provide an insight into how libraries are gathering and analysing data both locally and from across external, enterprise systems to demonstrate the value that they bring to the wider life of the institution and the success of its students and researchers. The chapter focuses on the work of three university libraries that are leading the way in demonstrating their impact in the lives of the students and other users of their services. The three case studies from the UK, US and Australia provide an insight both into what the data reveals and on the approaches they took to gather and analyse the data. They also highlight the technical, cultural and ethical challenges that the libraries faced in bringing this data together, and how they each overcame these barriers to change the way in which the library is viewed within the wider organization.

The three international case studies are:

- CASE STUDY 3.1 Stone, G., *Library impact data: investigating library use and student attainment* (University of Huddersfield), p. 51
- CASE STUDY 3.2 Nackerud, S., Fransen, J., Peterson, K. and Mastel, K., *Retention, student success and academic engagement at Minnesota* (University of Minnesota), p. 58
- CASE STUDY 3.3 Cox, B. and Jantti, M., *The Library Cube: revealing the impact of library use on student performance* (University of Wollongong), p. 66

Does library use have an impact on student success?

In 1968 Lloyd and Martha Kramer (Kramer and Kramer, 1968, 310) asked an apparently straightforward question: Does a student's use of the college library have a relationship to the likelihood of that student completing her course and graduating?

Such a question appears somewhat unnecessary. Of course it does – doesn't it?

As it happens, the Kramer paper suggests that there is a statistically significant correlation between library use and 'student persistence'. But, more importantly, the Kramers' and a small handful of other early studies (such as Barkey, 1965, who explored the impact of the library on a student's grade point average), had wanted to provide evidence to back up the intuitive responses such questions usually inspire. They wanted to use the data from the library and other parts of the university (such as the university's registry) to explore whether there was indeed a correlation between library use and student attainment and retention.

So the desire to use data to determine the impact and value of the library isn't new. However, despite the promise of such early enquiries, for the majority of libraries and their institutions, impact and value were demonstrated through techniques such as satisfaction surveys, both locally and nationally (the National Student Survey, or NSS, being the most well known in the UK), and individual student and researcher feedback. These are, of course, valid tools, but they provide only a small part of the picture. More importantly, these methods also tend to lack the impact of hard numbers and data. This is especially important for presentations to senior managers, who use the data to decide on the allocation of budgets and precious resources.

Data on the impact and value of the library is no longer a 'nice to have'; it is an essential management resource.

Taking analytics seriously

Libraries across the different sectors, as well as archives, museums and galleries, face unprecedented challenges, from financial and technological pressures, through to social and cultural changes more generally; and libraries, as well as academic and cultural institutions more widely, are increasingly expected to demonstrate the value they bring to students and users.

Yet, the library, like other cultural heritage institutions, is often considered to be of societal or cultural value, and these are values which are difficult to measure and often resist definition by numbers.

Over the last few years libraries, and in particular academic libraries, have been developing more sophisticated and data-driven approaches to demonstrating the impact of their services and resources to the institution and beyond. During the last two decades an increasing amount of literature has been published on the impact of libraries on their users – literature that uses data to demonstrate the value of libraries to their users. This work has explored the relationship between the library and its resources and the performance of the students. Early work took place in an environment where print was still dominant (De Jager, 2002) and at a time when extracting and sharing data from library and institutional systems was difficult and time consuming. Some researchers, from the public library sector (Sin and Kim, 2008; Suaiden, 2003), explored the wider societal impacts of libraries and demographic usage patterns.

From around 2010 onwards there was a resurgence of interest in data-driven strategy and analytics within the academic library sector. In particular there was significant and ground-breaking work by universities in the UK, US and Australia (the case studies below are brought together for the first time) to see how the myriad data that flowed through the library and wider institution could be harnessed for the benefit of students and researchers.

These analytic experiments share a number of features which differentiate them from earlier work and, to an extent, from the work taking place in other library sectors:

1 *Diversity of data*: The libraries are interested in data from across the library's systems and services (gate count, e-resource usage, computer logins), as well as data from across the institution (student records, student services, registry, IT). Individually, a dataset may appear peripheral or unimportant; as part of a larger collection, each dataset becomes significantly more important.
2 *Actionable analysis*: Data should not be collected for the sake of collecting it. Instead, it should contribute to a new insight or understanding that can be acted upon to improve the service or system for the user.
3 *Service development*: The analysis of the data isn't just about improving the experience of users of existing services, but also about providing a basis for new types of services and interventions. These new services can be more intimately tailored to the needs of users or groups of users, thus increasing the value of the services and of the library overall.

This approach – diversity of data, actionable insights and a focus on service development – means that these pioneer libraries are using data to drive decision making. There is recognition that effort should be invested in acting on the data for the benefit of students and users, and not in the collection of that data. Such an approach also enables new insights and discoveries to emerge; the aggregation of data can lead to new insights that the individual datasets could not yield on their own or in conjunction with one or two others.

The library is becoming a critical partner in the wider, enterprise exploitation of analytics by academic and cultural heritage institutions. Here we see an emerging field of interest where the library is helping to lead the way and has a significant amount of expertise and experience to provide to the institution. The emergence of student analytics and, more embryonically, research analytics, places the library at the heart of the analytics agenda. As analytics becomes an important strategic driver for institutions, so the library finds itself ideally placed to lead and contribute in this area. And nowhere is this expertise and knowledge more important than in the legal and ethical implications of collecting and exploiting impact data.

The ethics of impact

One thing recognized by each of the three case studies included here is the complex and challenging legal and ethical environment surrounding the use of student and user data. In Chapter 6 we will explore in more depth the legal and ethical aspects of analytics, but it is worth briefly dwelling on one of the drivers for the libraries at the forefront of analytics: what are the implications of not utilizing student and user data for their benefit?

We often focus on the risks of analytics, but we need to be equally clear about the risks of not using student and user data. What if a student, after failing a course, approached the institution to ask why it hadn't done everything in its power to prevent him from failing? Why hadn't the library and the institution picked up on the student's behaviour and patterns? Why had there been no intervention?

If Amazon can make recommendations for books based on prior searching behaviour and the purchasing behaviour of others, or Google can tailor search results based on your previous searches, location and background information, why can't the institution tailor its services to the student's particular requirements? This may take the form of relatively superficial interventions, such as recommendations for further reading, or highlighting what resources the top student in a class is reading. Equally, it may take the form of red flags for students whose behaviour indicates that they have an increased risk of failure or of dropping out, or tailoring services for specific groups of students so that the services an institution provides are ultimately more equitable.

As libraries respond to the rapidly evolving information landscape, so the importance of being able to effectively gather, analyse and act on data will be ever more critical. As the three case studies below highlight, we are still very much in the infancy of this area, but the studies also demonstrate the leading role that libraries are playing in the use of data and analytics, and how this has the potential to transform the role and impact of the library in the eyes of its users and host institution.

CASE STUDY 3.1

Library impact data: investigating library use and student attainment (University of Huddersfield)
Graham Stone

Introduction and background
In 2009 the Computing and Library Services at the University of Huddersfield made a successful application for the Customer Service Excellence quality standard in order to investigate non/low usage of library resources with respect to distinct customer groups, investigated as part of an equality impact assessment.

The project looked at three main indicators:

- book loans, using data from the Library Management System
- access to e-resources, using click-throughs from the e-resource system
- access to the library building, using statistics from the gate-entry system.

The results of this analysis showed that, for all three indicators, non/low usage ranged from 30% to 50% over a four-year period. At this point it was suggested that there would be potential to investigate the relationship between usage and final student grades. After negotiation with colleagues in Student Services it was agreed to combine this data with final grades for full-time undergraduate students. Data for attainment and usage between 2005/6 and 2008/9 was also examined.

After eliminating potential anomalies such as distance learners, postgraduates, part-time students and courses with low numbers where anonymity could not be guaranteed, the team began to see a relationship between usage and attainment for both e-resources usage and library borrowing.

At this point, however, the data had not yet been tested for statistical significance and it was therefore not known if the experience at Huddersfield was a function of the sample data used, rather than a true reflection of a relationship existing in the wider population.

The Library Impact Data Project
In late 2010 the University of Huddersfield, along with seven partners – University of Bradford, De Montfort University, University of Exeter, University of Lincoln, Liverpool John Moores University, University of

Salford and Teesside University – was awarded funding as part of the Jisc Information Environment Programme 2009–11 (Jisc, 2011) for the Library Impact Data Project (LIDP).

The original project, running from February to July 2011, aimed to use the original framework of the non-/low-usage research at Huddersfield to support the hypothesis that:

> There is a statistically significant correlation across a number of universities between library activity data and student attainment.

It is important to note that the project acknowledged from the outset that the relationship between the two variables is not a causal relationship and that other factors will also influence student attainment. Ultimately, the project's goal was to use the results to assist the wider higher education community by creating a better understanding of the link between library activity data and student attainment, and therefore to encourage greater use of library resources and contribute to improvements in student attainment.

Phase 1 of LIDP was also required to create a number of blog posts throughout its duration; the team chose to do this in a series of tagged blog posts from the project blog (University of Huddersfield, 2013; Stone, Ramsden and Pattern, 2011a). This approach proved invaluable and was adopted for the second stage of the project too.

Towards the end of 2011, the project team was approached by Jisc to put together a proposal for a second phase. Phase 2 aimed to build on the original project by digging deeper into the data. The team was asked to test to see whether there was a relationship between library usage and other variables such as demographic data and discipline – essentially, to start looking into possible causal factors in the data and to see which factors carried the most weight.

Analysing the data

The first phase of LIDP looked at 33,074 students across the eight university partners. The project anticipated potential issues with data collection, due to the size of the sample and the number of partners. Therefore, a minimum requirement of two out of the three indicators of library use was requested alongside final degree classification. It was felt that this would reduce the risk to the project and that partners would at least be able to provide one set of data to be used.

Phase 2 concentrated on 2,000 undergraduate students based at the main Huddersfield campus who were awarded a final grade in July 2011. For these students additional data, including demographic data, discipline and final results, was extracted from Huddersfield's student record system. This additional data built upon that collected in the original study and is shown in Table 3.1.

Table 3.1 *Dimensions of usage (Stone and Collins, 2013)*

Measure	Notes	Years
Number of items borrowed		Three
Number of library visits		Three
Hours logged into library PC	The way the system records this means that '1 PC hour' indicates that the student was logged into the computer at least once during a single hour on a single day.	Two
Hours logged into e-resources	As for hours logged into library PC	One
Number of PDF downloads		One
Number of e-resources accessed	Individual e-resources are determined by Huddersfield's systems and range from individual journal subscriptions to large journal platforms.	One
Number of e-resources accessed 5 or more times		One
Number of e-resources accessed 25 or more times		One
Percentage of e-resource usage occurring on campus	Using total number of e-resource logins	One

Information on the specific methodology used for Phase 1 was released as part of the LIDP toolkit (Stone, Ramsden and Pattern, 2011b) and this methodology was further refined in Phase 2 (Stone and Collins, 2013; Collins and Stone, 2014). In addition, the data from Phase 1 was released as an anonymized dataset under an Open Data Commons licence (Pattern, 2011).

Findings from the original project

Phase 1 of LIDP successfully demonstrated that there was a positive relationship between both book borrowing and e-resource usage and final degree result, 'Thus, the more a book or e-resource is utilized; the more likely a student is to have attained a higher level degree result' (Stone and Ramsden, 2013). At the time, the project could not show a correlation, due to the use of non-continuous data. However, the Huddersfield data was revisited in further work done by the project where use of grade point average was used to show a correlation. This research concurred with that of Wollongong and Minnesota.

Interestingly, the new data suggested that breadth of reading, which was indicated by the number of different e-resources used, might be a particularly important factor in degree success.

The hypothesis was supported by the borrowing and e-resource data from all institutional partners that supplied these two categories of data. However, it was found that there was no statistical significance between gate entry and attainment. In Huddersfield's case this was because Student Services were also located in the Library at the time of the study, meaning that a student might be entering the building for a number of different reasons. The same was true for those partner institutions where cafés, lecture rooms and social spaces were also part of the library.

The project was aware that both e-resource usage, e.g. EZproxy or Athens logins, and loan figures do not guarantee that a resource has been read and understood; however, as an indicator they could be benchmarked across the different institutions.

Phase 1 of the project also acknowledged that 'The amount of data used to prove a relationship is very large, and thus is more susceptible to demonstrating a relationship' (Stone and Ramsden, 2013). The project recommended that future studies should examine data at school or course level. Phase 2 did exactly that, investigating demographics, discipline and other sources of data such as retention.

Demographics

Phase 2 began by looking at demographic data (Table 3.2) to test whether there was a statistical significance between this and undergraduate usage (Stone and Collins, 2013).

The data showed that there were differences in use, for example:

Table 3.2 *Demographic data examined in Phase 2*	
Demographic	**Categories**
Age	Mature (aged 21 or over on entry) Non-mature
Gender	Men Women
Ethnicity	Asian Black Mixed Chinese Other
Country of domicile (the place where students live when they are not at university)	New EU Old EU China Rest of world

- mature students tend to have higher e-resource usage
- younger students are more likely to visit the library

- women show higher usage than men for resources use, but visit the physical library less
- Black and Asian students visit the library more often than White students and have higher PC usage and a higher proportion of their e-resource use occurs on campus
- Chinese students borrow fewer items than UK students and also use fewer e-resources.

The study found that, in general, the effect sizes were small; however, they did indicate a relationship between demographic factors and library usage and that the research supported the findings at Wollongong (Cox and Jantti, 2012).

Discipline

Phase 2 of LIDP also looked at the relationship between discipline and library usage. To do this, the project grouped the 105 full-time undergraduate courses at Huddersfield into six categories, with smaller sub-categories (Table 3.3). This allowed comparison across the six categories and within each category,

Table 3.3 *Discipline variables (Collins and Stone, 2014)*

High-level group	Subject groups	Number of courses included
Science	Science	3
Health	Nursing	5
	Health	7
Computing and engineering	Computing	13
	Engineering	6
Arts	Music	5
	Architecture	2
	Fashion	7
	2D Design	3
	3D Design	4
Humanities	English	2
	Drama	2
	Media and journalism	6
Social sciences	Business, management and accountancy	22
	Law	2
	Behavioural sciences	9
	Social work	3
	Education	4

although sub-categories could not be compared in this way. In some cases there were no sub-categories, due to the courses taught at Huddersfield.

The project found that the social sciences group was a significantly higher user than the other groups and the arts group was the lowest user for e-resources and PDF downloads (this perhaps reflects the way arts students use the library, particularly the physical resources).

Within the main categories, behavioural sciences was the highest user in the social sciences group. Business had higher usage than law, social work and education, but borrowed fewer items. Lawyers are extremely low users of library resources.

The full set of results from the study of discipline differences can be found on the LIDP project blog (University of Huddersfield, 2013).

Retention

The project also looked at the relationship between retention and library usage. A cumulative measure of usage for the first two terms of the 2010–11 academic year was examined. This allowed all users (particularly first-years) time to use the library's resources and establish usage patterns (otherwise a student who used nothing and dropped out in week two would skew the data). Thus, all students included in the study were at the university during the first two terms, and all had the same opportunity to accumulate usage.

The study found very similar results to the original project, i.e. a significant relationship between e-resource usage and book borrowing and student retention. This does not mean that non/low use leads to dropping out, but that there is a relationship. Therefore non/low use may be an indicator of the relationship between low/non-use and students dropping out; in the same way that a drop in attendance can be a sign of possible retention problems.

Further research

Over the course of the project, statistical significance was shown for the relationship between library usage and student attainment and retention. Differences were also recorded for certain groups. However, these results are merely an indicator; they do not tell us the reasons for the differences.

Further work is required at Huddersfield to understand these differences. As part of both phases of the project a number of focus groups were held. In particular, a focus group with students from computing and engineering helped the project group to understand the behaviour of students in this group.

In some cases the data needs to be broken down further; for example, measuring age in only two groups does not go very far towards explaining any possible behaviour.

However, the study did provide some useful intelligence for some of the bigger groups, most notably on discipline and country of domicile. The results imply that, given the link between usage and attainment, students in disciplines (and particularly their sub-categories) exhibiting low use could be targeted by subject librarians. The results certainly imply that a one-size-fits-all approach is inappropriate for information-literacy sessions and that library analytics can enhance the understanding of student behaviour.

The project concluded by suggesting that, as in Phase 1 of LIDP, it would be useful to replicate Phase 2 with data from a wider range of universities.

Shining a light on the LIDP

During both phases of LIDP, data extraction and processing took as long as four months. Clearly, if this is to become a regular exercise rather than a project, it will be necessary to automate the process as much as possible. Towards the end of Phase 2 of LIDP, Huddersfield and Mimas collaborated on a library analytics survey to understand any potential demand for a data analytics service which could enhance business intelligence at an institutional level to support strategic decision making, and whether there was any appetite for a shared-service approach to processing the raw data and providing analytics tools and data visualizations back to local institutions. The survey received 66 replies from library staff, including many library directors. Of those who replied, 96% confirmed that they would want automated provision of analytics demonstrating the relationship between student attainment and library usage within their institution, and 94.6% wanted to benchmark their data with other institutions. Furthermore, 87.7% were interested in the richer data that was used as part of Phase 2, e.g. discipline, age, year, nationality and grade.

The key strategic drivers for the use of library analytics that were identified by the library survey were, perhaps unsurprisingly:

1   enhancing the student experience
2   demonstrating value for money
3   supporting research excellence.

A subsequent meeting of representatives from the LIDP and Copac projects, JISC, SCONUL and RLUK decided that there was sufficient evidence demonstrating the need and desire for a shared analytics service. This resulted in the funding of the Library Analytics and Metrics Project (LAMP) (Jisc, 2013). The project is a partnership between JISC, Mimas and the University of Huddersfield.

Conclusion

The original LIDP was a very successful partnership between the eight collaborators, and this in itself was a success story, showing that a number of very different institutions could retrieve and share data in a very short space of time. LAMP is also very much a collaboration between a number of universities. During both LIDP and LAMP, international contacts were made with Wollongong and Minnesota, as three projects were following very similar paths. For LIDP this culminated in a joint presentation with Minnesota colleagues at Wyoming (Oakleaf et al., 2013). The LAMP project is also liaising with both Wollongong and Minnesota, with a view to finding common themes.

CASE STUDY 3.2

Retention, student success and academic engagement at Minnesota (University of Minnesota)

Shane Nackerud, Jan Fransen, Kate Peterson and Kristen Mastel

In the fall of 2011, staff at the University of Minnesota Libraries – Twin Cities Libraries began a project to measure how often and in what ways students used the Libraries' services and resources and to determine what kind of impact that usage had on students' academic success. Partnering with the University's Office of Institutional Research, the team investigated ways to match library service usage to individual user accounts – while retaining patron privacy – to determine who was and who was not using the library. During the initial phase of the project the team gathered library usage data for 13 different access points. After analysis of this data, the project team found that the majority of undergraduate and graduate students make use of library resources and services and that there is a strong association between library usage and higher student grade point averages (GPA) and retention. This case study discusses data-gathering techniques, analysis and the impact this project has had at the University of Minnesota Libraries and the University in general.

How we gather the data

This project began in the summer of 2011, when four University of Minnesota librarians came together to discuss how we could better measure student usage of library resources and services and how we could correlate library use to student success measures such as GPA and retention. We were able to accomplish both these goals because of partnerships created along the way, a willingness to be creative in deciding how to deal with privacy implications and a commitment from project team members and library administration to gather the data necessary and see this project through.

We wanted our picture of student usage to be as complete as possible. That meant gathering as much library transactional data as possible, in as many different areas as possible: electronic/digital, circulation, instruction and reference services. In addition, since we wanted both to measure demographic usage and to make associations to student success, we needed to retain personally identifiable user information. At the University of Minnesota (U of M) this means keeping the U of M student internet ID with record transactions; this is the same ID the students use to access their university e-mail and registration services.

Every librarian audience we speak to about our work eventually asks about privacy. How do we gather all this data but still retain an acceptable level of user privacy? This was one of the first issues we had to overcome in order to both gather the data necessary and analyse it. To conduct a project like this, personally identifiable user data must be retained. In our case, not only did we have to retain it, but we had to share it with another campus entity, the Office of Institutional Research.

Typically, a library will keep specific library usage data but not keep track of the actual patrons making use of the library resource or service. For example, a library will keep track of usage of a specific database, but the identities of who made use of that resource are not retained. For this study, in order to maintain user privacy to the extent possible, we decided to flip how a library typically tracks this data. Instead of tracking specific library resource usage, we keep specific user information (the U of M internet ID) and tie it to very general library resource usage. For example, when a user logs into a database we capture and retain their internet ID and the fact that they have logged into a database, not the actual database used or queries executed. We used this methodology for all 13 library access points from which we gathered data.

Library usage/access points

We grouped the 13 different library access areas into five main categories:

Digital access
- *Database, e-book, and e-journal logins*: Use of all three of these digital resources is captured through a 'click-through' script that captures user information, i.e. the U of M internet ID, before launching users into the University's installation of EZproxy.

- *Website logins*: The U of M uses the Drupal content management system, through which the Libraries capture user login information using the Drupal registration module. Users typically log in to access account information, saved resources and database and e-journal recommendations.

Circulation

- *Loans*: Check-outs and renewals are extracted from the University's Ex Libris Aleph catalogue transaction records. For the analysis, no distinction is made between initial check-out and renewal. In this project, loan data is requested at the end of each semester.
- *Interlibrary loans*: Interlibrary loan (ILL) transactions are managed through the University's instance of ILLiad, an ILL management system provided and hosted by OCLC. In this project ILL data is requested at the end of each semester.

Workstation usage

- *Workstations*: Users must log into the majority of computer workstations within the U of M Libraries through a shared computer management service called CybraryN™. Login data includes internet ID and is extracted from the CybraryN database at the end of each semester.

Instruction

- *Workshops*: The Libraries host in-person workshops throughout the year. Students, faculty and staff can register for these free workshops through the Libraries' Drupal registration module. Registration information, including internet ID, is extracted from Drupal.
- *Course-integrated instruction*: Subject liaison librarians frequently deliver in-class library instruction for faculty and courses that request this service. Staff pull the class list for each of these and add internet IDs for registered students to the dataset. This is the most time-consuming of the data that we gather in this project.
- *Introduction to Library Research workshops*: The Introduction to Library Research workshop or tutorial is typically taken in conjunction with the first-year writing course. Internet IDs are collected when students attend a face-to-face workshop or complete an online worksheet built into the online tutorial.

Reference

- *Peer Research Consultations*: With the Peer Research Consultant service, trained undergraduates help students to narrow down their research topic, use library resources and work on important research skills. Internet IDs are harvested from appointment lists.
- *Online reference*: The U of M Libraries do not collect internet ID information for questions asked at library reference desks. For this study, the group extracts internet IDs on reference transactions from OCLC QuestionPoint™.

So far, data has been collected in these areas for a total of four semesters. The bulk of analysis has been conducted on the fall 2011 semester data. For the fall 2011 semester we were able to gather approximately 1.5 million library transactions for the five categories above. Digital transactions were the dominant form of library use, at 1,110,727 transactions, followed by circulation (269,655), workstation usage (159,316), instruction (5,264) and reference (3,247). Subsequent semester numbers have seen steady increases in most of these categories, but have remained relatively consistent.

What does the data tell us?

Because we capture the U of M internet ID for all the library transaction types that we track, we are able to conduct analysis that reveals demographic information about our users, as well as correlations between library use and student success measures such as GPA and retention. Here, our partnership with the U of M Office of Institutional Research (OIR) is key. OIR has the tools and expertise to make short work of our raw data. Without OIR's expertise and interest in this project, we would not have been able to answer our main research question: Does library use have a positive effect on student success? Shortly after receiving our data, OIR analysts were able to extract the following significant results, and more.

Demographic data

OIR was able to tell us that approximately 77% of undergraduates and 85% of graduate students made use of the Libraries at some time during the fall 2011 semester. We also found that no college or professional school dropped below 60% for undergraduate and graduate student usage of the libraries. One professional school, the School of Pharmacy, saw 100% usage for the students in the programme. Obviously, we were excited by these numbers.

Because we retained type of usage in addition to counts, we could get a sense of how students in different colleges used different aspects of the

Libraries. For example, both undergraduates and graduate students in our College of Design make the most use of our physical collection, at 34% and 90%, respectively. At 74%, undergraduates from the College of Human Development make the most use of our digital collections, while only 47% of undergraduates in the College of Science and Engineering do the same. Overall, graduate students are the heaviest users of the Libraries for almost every college and school, except the Carlson School of Management (CSOM), where 74% of CSOM undergraduates used the libraries, as opposed to 67% of graduate students. There are a myriad of ways to slice and dice the data we have received, but overall the most exciting development is that we are finally able to gauge student usage of our resources and services by college, school, department and major.

This demographic analysis has also shed light on the GPAs of library users in contrast to their peers who have not used the library. Over the course of the four semesters that we have conducted this study, undergraduate students who used the library at least once in any of the library access points consistently had higher semester GPAs than students who made no use of the library. For example, students in the College Liberal Arts who made use of the Libraries had an average GPA of 3.13, while students in that college who did not use of the Libraries had an average GPA of 2.86. Obviously, this rudimentary fact does not necessarily tell us that these higher GPAs are *because* of library use. For that, we again relied on the expertise of our OIR to help us create a correlative analysis that moved us closer to answering the question: Does library use have an impact on student success?

Student success data and analysis

Of course, correlation does not mean causation. However, revealing associations within the data is an important part of establishing the Libraries' value to the University. With OIR, we decided to examine first-year non-transfer students to determine the association between the library interactions above, student retention and student academic achievement in the form of increased GPA. We looked only at first-year students because this eliminated some potentially confounding variables when considering sophomores, juniors and seniors that might influence our dependent measures of GPA and retention rates. For the fall semester of 2011, the total number of first-year non-transfer students was about 5,400.

About 71% of the students in this group made use of the libraries during the fall semester of 2011. Controlling for the effects of as many demographic, college environment and academic variables as we could, we found that, for this group, using the library at least once was associated with a .23 increase in a student's GPA, other factors being constant. Consider two students who are otherwise equal according to our measurable variables. If the non-library user has a GPA of 3.0, according to our model the library user is likely to have a GPA of 3.23. In addition, a one-unit increase in the types of use, or the more different interactions a student had with the library, was associated with a .07 increase in GPA per unit increase in usage.

Concerning retention, students who used the library once during the fall semester were 1.54 times more likely to re-enroll the following semester. Taking frequency into account, for every one-unit increase in the types of library use, students were 1.1 times more likely to re-enroll in the spring semester. In other words, the more different types of interactions a student has with the library, the better. Furthermore, we found that students who took the 'Introduction to Libraries II' library tutorial were 7.58 times more likely to re-enroll in the next semester.

In general, this study has provided very compelling evidence for the importance of libraries in first-year students' academic achievement and retention: first-year non-transfer students who used the U of M Libraries in their first semester had higher GPAs and retention rates, when controlling for additional factors. This is exciting news and can have a profound effect on the perception of library value in an academic setting.

Impact of the study

As one might expect, one of the first things we did with this data was to use it as evidence for continued or increased library budgetary support. The data was shared broadly with university administration and deans, but, interestingly, some administrators were unsurprised – at least on the surface – that library users were better students. It is somewhat obvious that library users will be more successful academically. However, because the correlations that we found were so strong, even when controlling for so many other academic markers, we have also found many other opportunities to use the results to reframe conversations between librarians and our stakeholders.

With our published work to back us up, we now come to our audiences armed with concrete statements and convincing charts. It is always interesting to ask faculty about their assumptions of student library use. When they ask 'What percentage of undergraduates used the libraries this semester?' the replies vary from 8% to 100% and everything in between. We shared our results at a number of events in 2013, including the bi-annual Focusing on the First Year Conference (attended by academic advisors and student affairs professionals) and at the First Year Writing Instructors Symposium (attended by 60+ instructors of First Year Writing programmes). We also were part of a professional development event for the University's Academic Advising Network. Depending on the audience, we have tied our results with Project

Information Literacy (http://projectinfolit.org/) to create an even more compelling case regarding the difficulties students have with academic research, the student success and retention benefits and the role of the Libraries in supporting students and academic research.

Many colleges at the University have developed one-credit first-year experience courses for new students. This is one of the high-impact practices identified by the Association of American Colleges and Universities, tied to improving student success and retention (www.aacu.org/leap/hip.cfm). We used the results of this data as the rationale for building a Libraries experience into the course. Many departments on campus want to be included in this type of compulsory course. Armed with our student success data, we were able to make a convincing case to the planning team of the College of Liberal Arts course, and in the fall of 2013 the Libraries piloted a customized mini-workshop and tour for about 500 students in the course.

Liaison librarians strive to connect with students in their assigned departments, but at a large university direct interaction with each student is difficult to accomplish. However, there is a group of people that we identified who do have that direct interaction: the academic advisors. At the U of M, undergraduates are advised primarily by professional staff rather than faculty. Academic advisors work at a college level and are well versed in helping students to develop strategies for academic success. A casual conversation with a group of academic advisors about our work has led to a pilot project which will provide the advisors with information on a student's library use, alongside their current schedule and past grades. This information will provide potential talking points for advisors, and increase their awareness of the different services the Libraries provide for students.

We also continue to work on ways that we can share our results with our actual users. In fall 2013, we began to formulate this into a communication strategy with new students. A library display used at recruiting events, and that features a graph of GPA vs. ACT (American College Testing) score for first-year students, draws in parents who want to know more about how we can help their students to start off on the right foot in college and how the library has changed since they themselves were undergraduates. Guides provided to incoming freshmen highlight the potential impact of different types of library use on GPA. We used the following messages both on our introductory page and in the book that new and transfer undergraduates receive during their orientation:

> Students who used the Libraries at least once in 2011–12 were twice as likely to return to the University for a second semester and had a higher average GPA than those who did not.

> (https://www.lib.umn.edu/about/guide)

Although it is difficult to measure the impact of these promotional messages, they have allowed us to craft a much stronger communication than before.

Because the data collected can be aggregated by academic department, library liaisons have had the opportunity to show faculty how their students' use of the library compares with that of their peers in other departments. For example, only 46% of undergraduates in one engineering major used the Libraries over the course of the spring 2012 semester. This rate by itself was not compelling to faculty: they don't expect their students to use library services much. However, when they compared their students' usage to the 63% of undergraduates in the College of Science and Engineering who used the Libraries in the same semester, the conversation changed. The library liaison was invited to teach a session for the department's senior design class for the first time in the fall of 2012, and the spring 2013 usage rate rose to 57%.

The data we have collected may even impact on library spaces. We have recently begun planning for both short-term and long-term renovations in the largest libraries on campus. We came back to our data gathered for this project, but realized that, due to our deliberate focus on usage (e.g. we know who used the libraries in x way but we don't know the specific book, database, e-journal, etc.) it wasn't useful to determine who uses specific libraries. In a pilot project, we took data on our computer workstation logins from just one location and, with the help of OIR, we were able to get one measure of who was using one of our physical spaces, with a breakdown of specific colleges or departments. As for many libraries, with the vast majority of our use being online, we need to build a more accurate picture of how and why patrons are using our spaces and what spaces and services will attract new ones. We will continue to mine, reuse and repurpose the data to help build this picture.

Conclusion

We continue to look for ways to incorporate our data and findings into our communication strategy, outreach, library planning and decision making. We plan to continue this study into future semesters and possibly to create a longitudinal analysis of a complete four-year student cohort. We also continue to look for different research questions that this data can help to answer, in order, hopefully, to change service offerings or create new ones, or even to help us decide when services are no longer needed. Overall we are pleased with the results of this project so far, but we realize that with continuing persistence and expanded efforts this data has the potential to do much more. The power of this study is that it demonstrates that libraries can successfully pull together a relatively complete picture of library use, create the campus partnerships necessary to make sense of the data, get a better sense of who uses their resources and services and correlate that use to actual student success. We are committed to continuing this project and we are eager to discover new ways to use this data and expand the impact of the study.

CASE STUDY 3.3

The Library Cube: revealing the impact of library use on student performance (University of Wollongong)

Brian Cox and Margie Jantti

Introduction

This case study describes how the University of Wollongong Library (UWL), in partnership with the University's Performance Indicator Unit, partnered to build new data and reporting models to join library usage data with students' demographic and academic performance data to test correlations and to ultimately create a new narrative. It is a discourse on the contribution of the library to the student experience and their academic success.

Constructing the problem statements

The proliferation of information via services external to the library, e.g. the internet, has resulted in a seismic shift in how libraries are used. Students have unprecedented choice in the source, content and format of learning materials they use, and can effectively bypass the library. These wide-ranging choices have, in effect, repositioned the student from being an active, though still highly dependent, learner into a consumer of information. This shift in behaviour comes with a learning cost, and has become a battle that is fought daily in tutorial classes and lectures, as academics and librarians try to encourage students to make better use of the high-quality sources of information acquired or subscribed to by the library (at considerable cost). For these reasons, it is more important than ever for libraries to demonstrate to students and other stakeholders the value of using the library's resources and services. The challenge, however, is that the value delivered by libraries is often considered to be social, educational or cultural, and these are values which are difficult to measure.

For the academic library, a key focus is on the transformative power of information; and the question to be answered is: does a student's academic performance improve as a result of using information resources made available by the library; what does the student receive for their investment of time and energy spent in using library resources and services? (Neal, 2011; Stone and Ramsden, 2013). At UWL, we lacked ongoing valid and reliable data collection from both library and enterprise systems, which prevented us from making supported assertions about the value provided by the Library. What was needed was a cost-effective, reliable and sustainable way of collecting information on the Library's impact on student outcomes.

The genesis of the UWL Cube centred on the examination of two significant and interrelated problems facing academic libraries. Firstly, many libraries are under mounting pressure to demonstrate value in the context of:

- economic adversity (and accountability)
- the intensification of competition for students.

Secondly, libraries are increasingly being challenged to provide compelling evidence that directly links information resources and engagement activities to positive outcomes for their clients. Libraries that do not provide such evidence will be at increasing risk of having their funding either reduced or eliminated (Jantti and Cox, 2013; Soria, Fransen and Nackerud, 2013a).

Sound marketing, inter alia, should improve a library's value proposition, and being able to articulate strong evidence of value enhances a library's ability to effectively market itself. Yet, for many libraries, the lack of access of up-to-date business intelligence is a barrier to identifying which segments of their client base are not using their resources and services (Soria, Fransen and Nackerud, 2013b). Without this information, academic libraries cannot identify in an accurate and timely manner:

- whom to target through communications and engagement initiatives
- whether such activities have increased their market share of information consumers.

Consequently, a lack of evidence linking clients' library usage to positive client outcomes can lead to a cycle of devaluation, as poor evidence of value leads to weak marketing impact, leading in turn to poorer usage, which then reduces the value offered by the library as the cost per client increases. Breaking this cycle is of paramount importance to the long-term survival of academic libraries. For both problems the issue is a lack of collecting ongoing valid and reliable data from which generalizations can be made about the value provided by the library.

UWL, through the Library Cube, has produced the information which it needs to unambiguously demonstrate the contribution it is making to institutional learning, teaching and research goals. The Cube centres on the integration and interrogation of a series of discrete datasets, e.g. student performance, student attrition, student demographic data, and borrowing and electronic resources usage data. The Cube illustrates the correlation between usage of library resources and academic performance and demonstrates that those students who are non or low users of UWL information resources are at an academic disadvantage.

Creating the Library Cube

The University of Wollongong (UOW) has a Performance Indicators Unit (PIU) to provide senior staff with accessible and integrated reporting and analysis tools through a secure, web-based Performance Indicators Portal. PIU collects and leverages critical data through scorecard, reporting and analysis capabilities and provides a one-stop data source for institutional data.

In 2009, UWL began working with PIU to develop a tailored database and reporting function – the Library Cube – to link library usage data with students' demographic and academic performance data.

The main requirement for linking together any two datasets is that both should contain a common unique identifier. In our case, all of the systems required to create the Library Cube contain a unique personal identifier – the student number.

The two UWL data sources fed into the Library Cube include loans data and data relating to usage of electronic resources. Due to the limitations of UWL's Library Information Management System, the only usable data that can be exported that includes the student unique identifier is the total number of items borrowed to date. To build time-series data, an export of data occurs weekly, and the difference between two weeks is the borrowing activity that occurred each week.

UWL uses EZproxy logs (sourced from authentication) to extract information on usage of the Library's electronic resources. Each time a user accesses certain library resources, an entry is generated in the log file. These resources include subscription databases, e-books and e-readings materials, which can be accessed via the UWL catalogue or through links provided on UOW's learning management system.

Once exported, the data is held within an Oracle Data Warehouse, with access managed through an IBM Cognos business intelligence toolkit. The entire system is developed and maintained by PIU. Users have two options for viewing reports:

1   canned reports by faculty (providing predefined views)
2   highly customized reports, created by simply dragging and dropping the dimensions of the Library Cube, such as gender, faculty, country of origin, etc. either as a field in a cross-tab table or as a filter value. Users can also select what they wish to measure, such as student head-count or total number of borrowings.

The web-based system lets users slice and dice data easily, as well as save their views.

Limitations

Before we look at the relationship between usage of our resources and student performance, it is important that we acknowledge the following points:

- *Borrowing a book does not automatically translate into learning.* Even if the student has read the book, this does not mean that they have understood or used the book. The same logic applies to electronic resources.
- *There are many other factors besides the Library that contribute to students' academic success,* not the least of which are academic teaching skills and students' attitudes and aptitude.
- *Correlation does not prove cause.* For example, good teachers may encourage students to use the Library more frequently, and the correlation may therefore be a product of good teaching skills, rather than of engagement with the collection per se.
- *Other variables that may contribute to students' academic success,* such as attendance, either cannot or have not been captured in the Library Cube, due to technical and resource limitations.

There are, however, a number of factors that increase UWL's confidence in the validity of the findings, including the following:

- Sampling error is not a problem, as the data is a census, and a census that is collected weekly for loans and daily for electronic resources. Note: the Cube is updated weekly.
- There is very little variability within the categories over time.
- There is a very strong relationship between the average marks for each level of resource usage and student grades.

Finally, with a few notable exceptions, the relationship still holds for many views of the data.

How the Library Cube operates

Although PIU hosts a large historical dataset for UOW student demographics and grades, UWL began collecting resource usage data for integration into the Library Cube only in mid-2009 for loans and in January 2010 for online resources. Consequently, the Library Cube contains time-series data starting only from 2010.

The logs contain useful information, such as the students' unique identifiers, but they also contain a lot of extraneous data. Counting the number of log entries proved futile, as they vary wildly depending upon the online resource being accessed. UWL decided to use the timestamp in the log as a de facto time-session measure, using the following business rules:

- The day is divided into 144 10-minute sessions.
- If a student has an entry in the log during a 10-minute period, then 1/6 is added to the sum of that student's access for that session (or week, in the case of the 'Marketing' Cube).
- Any further log entries during that student's 10-minute period are not counted.

Using this logic, UWL measures how long students spent using its electronic resources with a reasonable degree of accuracy, due to the small time periods (10 minutes) being measured.

The primary ethical and legal issue is privacy. The UOW's Privacy Information Sheet outlines the 12 principles with which the University must comply regarding the collection, storage, access, use and disclosure of personal information. Fortunately, there are no legal barriers, as UOW has consent to use personal information for the project through its privacy consent framework, which students must agree to as part of their enrolment.

At an ethical level, the additional privacy risks potentially posed by the project have been eliminated by managing the personal information in a particular way. Privacy is an issue only to the extent that it involves the use and disclosure of personal information. UWL will not use the Cube to drill down to see a specific individual's personal information. That is, the data viewed in the Cube will always be aggregated. In all cases, the personally identifiable data that users can glean from the Cube is significantly less than that which can already be ethically and legally obtained through the library management system, logs and access to student management systems. Moreover, access to the Cube is even more restricted than is the case for the other systems that contain the same information.

Resource use and student performance

Examination of the earliest captured raw data showed that there were students who used UWL electronic resources who failed, and there were some non-users who performed strongly. However, all else being equal, the more that students used UWL's electronic resources, the more likely they were to perform better. At the time of conducting this level of analysis in 2010 only half of one per cent of the high users failed (0.47%), whereas 19% of non-users failed. In other words, non-users were 40 times more likely to fail than were high users of library electronic resources. The story was similar for loans, but not as dramatic.

Further analysis of the aggregated data does reveal a strong correlation between the use of UWL information resources and student grades. For example, the average mark for students who never used UWL electronic resources in 2013 was 59. The average mark for students who spent up to one hour per year accessing UWL electronic resources was 64. The chart in Figure 3.1 shows a very strong nonlinear relationship between average usage of resources and average student marks (R-squared = 0.82).

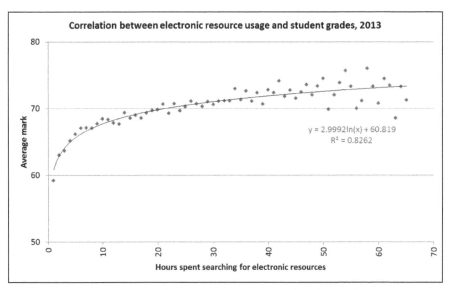

Figure 3.1 *Correlation between electronic resource usage and student grades*

We defined the first frequency to contain less than 20 students as a cut-off point (to exclude the long tail). These outliers constitute 1.8% of the total (579 out of 32,322 students). To apply a logarithmic line of best fit, we incremented each of the frequencies by one. This has no impact on the correlation, the line of best fit's shape, or the points' relationship to each other.

In 2013, the correlation between *borrowing* and student marks was less striking (R-squared = 0.64). The correlation was not as tight, and the increase in marks with usage was not as steep (Figure 3.2).

Table 3.4 illustrates the types of reports that both UWL and faculty can access and produce. The views outline the usage trends of undergraduate students from the Faculty of Business as well as the distribution of usage and impact in terms of the weighted average mark (WAM).

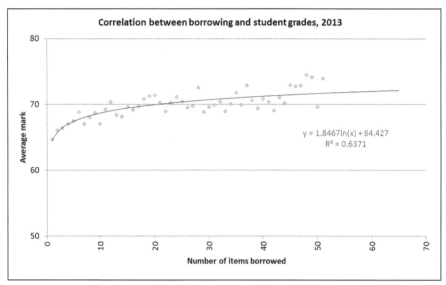

Figure 3.2 *Correlation between borrowing and student grades*

Table 3.4 *Weighted average marks (WAM) for undergraduate students (Faculty of Business) against annual electronic resource usage frequency (hours)*

Hours	Marks	Number of students
No Usage	57.1	1,651
1–5	63.6	2,652
6–10	67.1	824
11–20	68.6	627
21–40	70.0	280
41–80	76.5	42
Outliers		3
Annual electronic resource usage frequency (hours)	63.6	6,079

The Library Cube is now part of the UOW enterprise reporting system and went live in May 2012. Representatives from UWL and PIU have met with key stakeholders within the faculties to communicate the purpose, scope and functionality of its reports and views. Faculty members have welcomed access to another dataset that helps them to better understand the student experience and the Library's impact on student success.

Introducing a new conversation

Although the data illustrates the extent and impact of the Cube's use, it also poses many questions that will require further investigation, such as why some student groups are more successful than others when usage patterns are similar.

For example, our domestic[1] female students gain a lot more advantage from using resources than do their international[2] counterparts. Domestic female students who spent between 81 and 160 hours searching for electronic resources in 2013 scored 21 marks higher than non-users. However, in comparison, the gain for international female students was only 7 marks.

When looking at the difference in academic performance of students who do not use our resources, as compared to the heaviest users, the Faculty of Science, Medicine and Health gets the most out of electronic resources. The improvement from using electronic resources is striking. In 2013 the average weighted mark of non-users was 45, and rose steadily to a distinction (76) for students who spent between 81 and 160 hours searching for electronic resources.

The students of the Faculty of Law, Humanities and the Arts receive the highest benefit from books, while the Faculty of Business students receive the least benefit.

Another interesting finding is the relative benefit that postgraduate students gain from using the UWL collection, relative to undergraduates. Postgraduates gain significantly less benefit than do undergraduate students. Increased usage of the collection does not have anywhere near the same impact for our experienced students. This finding poses questions about the relevance of current approaches to information literacy support and how these skills could be promoted throughout a student's academic career to improve how much they benefit.

The Marketing Cube

The utility of the Library Cube is designed to be manifold, so as to provide the information needed to further support continuous improvement in three areas: collection development, academic relationships and marketing.

The Library spends a significant proportion of its budget in subscribing to electronic databases. We are able to obtain third-party information (e.g. counter statistics) on the number of downloads associated with subscriptions, and we combine this with cost data to create rough indices, such as cost per download. UWL uses this information, in consultation with academic staff, to continually improve and develop its collection.

For example, we will be able to provide academics with the evidence they need to effectively promote the Library to their students. We will also be able to draw on this information in our own teaching activities, to convincingly demonstrate the research behaviours that lead to academic success. We will know which specific group we should target to improve take-up. Most importantly, we will know almost immediately whether our marketing and engagement efforts have succeeded, which in turn will help us to make informed decisions about whether to change tack or continue with more of the same.

The Marketing Cube will be updated weekly, which will allow us to view in a much more timely fashion how our electronic resources are being used. We will also be able to see at the end of each session which resources had a significant impact on academic performance and which resources did not. We will be able to use this information to make better-informed decisions about collection development for electronic resources and to identify and replicate the processes that have led to specific resources facilitating higher academic performance.

Conclusion

The ability to demonstrate the value and impact of libraries and their collections is becoming increasingly important. Not only do we need to convince the university executives and faculty of the value of libraries; our most challenging audience is increasingly the student body. We now have a compelling story to share: based on the data generated to date, students who access UWL resources *do* outperform students who don't. The Library Cube, therefore, provides a new facet for better understanding the total student experience.

The time needed to establish the problem statement, business rules and reporting requirements has been lengthy, but ultimately worthwhile. The UWL Cube, the University of Huddersfield Library Impact Data and the University of Minnesota projects all provide insight on the types of datasets that can be considered and collected, and identify key collaborators (e.g. PIU) and the business rules or algorithms that can be applied. Libraries interested in pursuing a similar project are encouraged to talk to their enterprise data centres or units to identify the potential for linking discrete datasets. Enquiries and requests for further information on the UWL Cube can be directed to the authors of this case study.

Chapter conclusion: from knowing to showing!

Libraries and other cultural heritage institutions are increasingly moving from intuitively knowing about the impact and value they have on their students and users, into a paradigm where they are able to evidence that value. But this demonstration of value is not an end in itself for the libraries engaged in this innovative data collection. Rather, it forms part of an embedded and systematic approach to the collection and exploitation of data that enables them to be much more agile in the ways in which they respond to the needs of their users. Demonstrating value and impact means that libraries are collecting and acting upon the very data that can inform the improvement of collections and services, creating a positive feedback loop.

Such a data-centric approach to uncovering new narratives about the use and value of libraries begins to also highlight where the limitations of such an approach might be. While the numbers are important, they are not enough. Our next chapter begins to explore other approaches to library data and metrics which can begin to fill in some of the gaps that emerge as we become more comfortable with utilizing analytics in our libraries and institutions.

Library impact and value: further resources

If you'd like to find out more about the work described in this chapter, and access further reading and inspiration, below are additional resources for individuals and institutions interested in demonstrating library and organizational impact and value.

More on the case studies

- Library Impact Data Project (LIDP at Huddersfield), http://bit.ly/libimpact.
- Discovering the impact of library use and student performance (The Library Cube), http://bit.ly/libcube.
- Library data and student success (University of Minnesota), http://bit.ly/MinnImpact.

Additional resources

- Exploiting activity data in the academic environment, www.activitydata.org.
- Library analytics bibliography, http://bit.ly/analyticsbib.
- Educause Library Analytics Toolkit, www.educause.edu/library/analytics.

Notes

1 An Australian Citizen, Australian Permanent Resident or a New Zealand Citizen.
2 A student who is not a domestic student. This includes students on temporary residence visas.

References

Barkey, P. (1965) Patterns of Student Use of a College Library, *College Research Library*, March, **2**, 115–18.

De Jager, K. (2002) Successful Students: does the library make a difference? *Performance Measurement and Metrics*, **3** (3), 140–4.

Kramer, L. and Kramer M. (1968) The College Library and the Drop Out, *College Research Library*, July, **29**, 310–12.

Sin, S.-C. J. and Kim, K.-S. (2008) Use and Non-use of Public Libraries in the Information Age: a logistic regression analysis of household characteristics and library services variables, *Library & Information Science Research*, **30** (3), 207–15.

Suaiden, E. J. (2003) The Social Impact of Public Libraries, *Library Review*, **52** (8), 379–87.

Case Study 3.1

Collins, E. and Stone, G. (2014) Understanding Patterns of Library Use among Undergraduate Students from Different Disciplines, *Evidence Based Library and Information Practice*, **9** (3), 51–67.

Cox, B. L. and Jantti, M. (2012) Capturing Business Intelligence Required for Targeted Marketing, Demonstrating Value, and Driving Process Improvement, *Library and Information Science Research*, **34** (4), 308–16.

Jisc (2011) *Jisc Activity Data*, www.jisc.ac.uk/whatwedo/programmes/inf11/activitydata.aspx.

Jisc (2013) *Library Analytics and Metrics Project*, http://jisclamp.mimas.ac.uk.

Oakleaf, M., Stone, G., Pattern, D., Bowles-Terry, M., Peterson, K., Nackerud, S. and Fransen, J. (2013) Do or Do Not...There is No Try: the quest for library value. In *Association of College & Research Libraries Conference*, 10–13 April 2013, Indianapolis, Indiana.

Pattern, D. (2011) *Library Impact Data Project Data*, University of Huddersfield, http://eprints.hud.ac.uk/11543.

Stone, G. and Collins, E. (2013) Library Usage and Demographic Characteristics of Undergraduate Students in a UK Universit,. *Performance Measurement and Metrics*, **14** (1), 25–35.

Stone, G. and Ramsden, B. (2013) Library Impact Data Project: looking for the link between library usage and student attainment, *College and Research Libraries*, **74** (6), 546–59.

Stone, G., Ramsden, B. and Pattern, D. (2011a) Looking for the Link Between Library Usage and Student Attainment, *Ariadne*, **67**, www.ariadne.ac.uk/issue67/stone-et-al.

Stone, G., Ramsden, B. and Pattern, D. (2011b) *Library Impact Data Project Toolkit*, Manual, University of Huddersfield.

University of Huddersfield (2013) Library Impact Data Project, https://library3.hud.ac.uk/blogs/lidp.

Case Study 3.3

Association of College and Research Libraries (2010) *Value of Academic Libraries: a comprehensive research review and report,* researched by Megan Oakleaf, Chicago, Association of College and Research Libraries.

Counter – Counting Online Usage of Networked Electronic Resources (2014) www.projectcounter.org/.

Jantti, M. and Cox, B. (2010) Measuring the Value of Library Resources and Student Academic Performance through Relational Datasets, *Proceedings of the Library Assessment Conference: building effective, sustainable, practical assessment,* Baltimore, Maryland, 25–27 October 2010, http://libraryassessment.org/bm~doc/proceedings-lac-2010.pdf.

Jantti, M. and Cox, B. (2013) Measuring the Value of Library Resources and Student Academic Performance through Relational Datasets, *Evidence Based Library and Information Practice,* **8** (2), 163–71.

Neal, J. G. (2011) Stop the Madness: the insanity of ROI and the need for new qualitative measures of academic library success, *Proceedings of the ACRL 2011 Conference, a declaration of Interdependence,* Philadelphia, March 30–April 2, www.ala.org/ala/mgrps/divs/acrl/events/national/2011/papers/stop_the_madness.pdf.

Soria, K. M., Fransen, J. and Nackerud, S. (2013a) Analyzing Demographics: assessing library use across the institution, *Libraries and the Academy,* **13** (2), 131–45.

Soria, K. M., Fransen, J., and Nackerud, S. (2013b) Library Use and Undergraduate Student Outcomes: new evidence for students' retention and academic success, *Libraries and the Academy,* **13** (2), 147–64.

Stone, G. and Ramsden, B. (2013) Library Impact Data Project: looking for the link between library usage and student attainment, *College and Research Libraries,* **74** (6), 546-59.

UOW (2010) Privacy Information Sheet – General, www.uow.edu.au/content/groups/public/@web/@fin/@lcu/documents/doc/uow061010.pdf.

Going beyond the numbers: using qualitative research to transform the library user's experience

Chapter overview

In this chapter we turn our attention to ways of capturing and understanding more complex and difficult-to-measure variables, like the experience of using a service.

This chapter provides practical examples and techniques that have been used to gain a deeper understanding of user behaviours and motivations, both when interacting online and in the physical space of institutions and libraries. The two case studies in this chapter are about observing student and user behaviours, mapping the ways that they interact online and physically (with services, resources and each other) and how they use technology and space for learning and collaborating. The chapter highlights the increasing importance of this type of qualitative approach for understanding and shaping both the digital and physical spaces that students and users inhabit.

Two international case studies are featured in this chapter:

- CASE STUDY 4.1 Connaway, L. S., Hood, E. M. and Vass, C. E., *Utilizing qualitative research methods to measure library effectiveness: developing an engaging library experience* (OCLC), p. 82
- CASE STUDY 4.2 Lanclos, D., *Ethnographic techniques and new visions for libraries* (University of North Carolina, Charlotte), p. 96

Qualitative research and the user experience

When we talk about data helping to drive decision making in organizations we often assume that the kinds of data we're referring to are the 'hard' numbers: the number of users, the frequency of use and so on.

Yet, as organizations that deliver services and, more importantly, experiences, libraries, archives and cultural heritage institutions are ultimately interested in understanding the behaviours, motivations and needs of users. We want to be able not only to know what users do but also to understand what their experience is like.

Much of the current interest in this type of qualitative research in cultural and academic institutions has been driven by a number of factors, but central to these have been the technological changes that have transformed the information landscape. In particular, innovations in user experience – driven by digital companies and organizations – have radically changed the expectations and assumptions of anyone using online (and, indeed, physical) services.

Libraries and other cultural heritage institutions no longer have a monopoly on access to information or content, nor, critically, are they simply competing against similar or familiar organizations in providing access to that content or service. Rather, they are competing against wealthy, web-based and technology-astute companies. The rules have changed irrevocably.

In a digital information environment, where the user experience is key, the distinction between services provided by libraries and the technologies of companies like Microsoft, Amazon and Google is becoming blurred or disappearing entirely. There is an urgent need for traditional information and content providers to be able to ask more nuanced and complex questions, to explore subtle variables and to seek out new and emerging patterns in the data.

To gain these kinds of deeper insight organizations need to adopt a mixed-method approach to analytics, one that 'incorporate[s] inquiries that measure and count, as well as asking open-ended, descriptive or analytical questions' (Case Study 4.1). By the combination of both approaches the richness of the data is increased dramatically and what was once simply numbers now becomes a critical piece in a far more detailed jigsaw of user data.

But we can also go further, so that what is being described when we talk about a qualitative approach is also a rebalancing of the data and analytics methodology: a rebalancing that incorporates ways that enable the user to tell their own story. The role of the librarian, archivist or curator is to listen and, when appropriate, to question the narrative; this is, after all, an active dialogue with the user, not passive listening. As Donna Lanclos articulates in her ethnographic case study of two academic libraries:

> Crafting [library] policy is about constructing a compelling narrative, and qualitative analytics such as ethnographic data are tailor made for the grounded storytelling in which libraries and other parts of higher education need to engage so as to draw resources and attention to their value.
>
> (Case Study 4.2)

These dialogues are a key ingredient in being able both to improve and refine current services and systems and to identify potential new services and meet new or unmet user requirements – often meeting users' needs that they may not have fully realized they have, or at least that they have not fully articulated.

Qualitative research and emerging user needs

A mixed-methods approach, where both quantitative and qualitative approaches are taken, enables the service to understand both what the user actually does and the context for those actions and the experience that those interactions provide. This coalescence of data is incredibly powerful, both for understanding how current services are used and might be improved and also for articulating hidden or emerging needs and requirements that users themselves may not be entirely aware of.

The way we interact with a space may leave traces of a need that could never be fully articulated by the user. Yet, should that space be altered to meet that nascent need, the user's experience might be positively transformed.

Suddenly our metrics for success depend not just on numbers but also on a narrative from the user or visitor that includes words such as 'delightful', 'surprising' and 'amazing'.

To put it simply: the user is placed at the centre of our decisions and developments. Development of services is driven by the user, not by the requirements of the back office or by the processes that the service has always employed. The user sits at the centre of developments, whether they realize it or not.

Such an approach is relatively familiar (many institutions and organizations have adopted these types of approaches), yet still new. It requires a rethinking of priorities and the allocation of resources and – maybe most importantly of all – of the skills and talent required to deliver these kinds of developments and approaches.

A mix of skills and methodologies

As with quantitative data and analysis, cultural heritage institutions will need to think about the kinds of skill-sets that are required to take advantage of this kind of data and to develop new services. Some of these skill-sets might be brought in when needed or built up locally, or the two approaches could be combined. But having the right mix of skills and talent is essential in the cultural heritage sector so as to meet the constantly shifting demands of users both now and into the future.

This doesn't necessarily mean large amounts of expense or recruitment. Both of the case studies in this chapter describe methods that could be employed by almost any size of institution or organization. Academic libraries have an opportunity to use the skills of postgraduates in appropriate areas;

other organizations could make use of internships, residencies and so on. These may feel like fairly radical steps, yet elsewhere such roles are deeply embedded in the organizational culture.

The numbers of anthropologists and ethnographers employed by companies like Google and Microsoft now rival – and may even exceed – the numbers employed by governments, who have traditionally employed the largest numbers with these skills.

Growing numbers of employees with user experience (UX) skills are now working in digital companies as well as in government and other sectors (and are starting to emerge in the library and cultural heritage sectors). Their skill-sets have been critical in the development of the online, web-based software, applications and services that are beginning to permeate into those knowledge/information sectors where the transition to a digital environment continues.

In the cultural heritage sector these changes are still occurring relatively slowly, and having the right mix and availability of skills will ensure a certain amount of resilience. Such resilience is essential in an environment where there is no road map or other obvious transition from the way things are today to some future point. The disruptions faced today by libraries, archives, museums and galleries are not the exception, but an indication of the constant nature of change. The following two case studies begin to explore ways and strategies by which we can begin to embed approaches to gathering qualitative data into the day-to-day activities of our libraries and institutions.

CASE STUDY 4.1

Utilizing qualitative research methods to measure library effectiveness: developing an engaging library experience

Lynn Silipigni Connaway, (OCLC Research), Erin M. Hood (OCLC Research) and Carrie E. Vass (OCLC Research)

Introduction and justification for qualitative data collection methods

It is critical in the current environment for most institutions and organizations to justify their impact, due to funding challenges. Libraries and information organizations are not exempt from this. It may be more critical than ever for libraries to articulate their contributions to their communities. In order to demonstrate institutional value, library and information science (LIS) professionals must 'define outcomes of institutional relevance and then measure the degree to which they attain them' (Kaufman and Watstein, 2008, 227). Fact-based, data-driven cases must be presented and library-generated data can be leveraged to provide evidence to demonstrate value.

One way of measuring a library's impact is to conduct a user-centred evaluation of its services and systems. This approach requires the systematic collection and analysis of data that will identify how users get their information and engage with services and systems and how they perceive their satisfaction and dissatisfaction with services and systems (Connaway, forthcoming).

The evaluation of library services requires time, effort and financial investment from its organization or institution. Formal assessment is a rigorous, ongoing process that is data driven, evidence based and utilizes accepted research methods and data-collection techniques (Connaway and Radford, 2013).

Evaluation tools such as surveys and compiled statistics are pervasive in library science. Until recently, quantitative methods have predominated LIS research (Connaway and Powell, 2010; Connaway et al., forthcoming). Quantitative measures typically require a highly structured, problem-solving approach which relies on the quantification of concepts for purposes of evaluation and measurement (Glazier and Powell, 1992). However, conventional quantitative data that reports outputs (the number of books circulated, the number of reference questions answered, attendance at library-use or information-literacy instruction) and inputs (space, budget dollars, collections, equipment, staff) creates a narrow picture of performance (Connaway et al., forthcoming). While this type of reporting is convenient for describing items or services that are easily measured, other types of inquiry include information that cannot be measured statistically, requiring a different form of investigation and assessment.

Often, the questions that librarians want to ask about users' behaviours are complex and require multiple approaches, such as asking users directly about their behaviours and observing them. In these cases, it is worthwhile to design mixed-methods approaches that incorporate inquiries that measure and count, as well as asking open-ended, descriptive or analytical questions. Examples of more interpretive research questions that could be asked when evaluating services, sources and systems include: How do users determine whether or not a source is authoritative? What fluencies (digital, information and computer) are relevant to people's choices? What are the motives behind choosing one source or plan of action over another? (Connaway, Lanclos and Hood, 2013). The answers to these questions can provide LIS professionals with the knowledge, skills and confidence to develop user-centred library services and systems (Connaway, forthcoming). A well-planned mixed approach can generate a sophisticated, enlightened representation of an environment. The disadvantages of using a combined approach are that it is time consuming and involves large datasets that need to be triangulated.

An example of a mixed-methods research approach is the Visitors and Residents (V&R) project, funded by Jisc and OCLC and in partnership with the University of North Carolina (UNC) at Charlotte. This project utilizes both qualitative and quantitative research methods, with an emphasis on qualitative methods and data-collection tools, to provide a rich description of how users and prospective users of library services and systems get and use information and engage with technology, and to identify why they make the choices they do about technology, services and sources.

Description of the V&R project's multi-method research design

The V&R project is a three-year longitudinal project that follows a pre-selected group of individuals' progression through their academic lifecycles (White and Connaway, 2011–12). The project goals are to identify the technology and sources individuals adopt, in order to determine more effective ways for engagement between institutions such as libraries, their resources and services, and individuals.

The V&R model represents a continuum of behaviours that demonstrate engagement with technology, services and sources. Individuals' behaviours are more 'visitor' or more 'resident', depending on their motivations and the context of their need. A 'visitor' mode of behaviour can be demonstrated when individuals decide upon a goal or task to be achieved, select an online tool, complete the task and then log off. They leave no social trace of themselves online. A 'resident' mode of behaviour is demonstrated when individuals spend their time online and view the web as a place where they can express themselves and socialize. Residents will rely heavily on social networking platforms and maintain a digital identity which is locatable even when they are not online (Connaway, Lanclos and Hood, 2013).

The data-collection tools include semi-structured interviews with four different groups of individuals in different educational stages, diaries (a qualitative, ethnographic approach) and an online survey (White and Connaway, 2011–12). This design was selected to answer the project's specific research questions and to enable a cross-examination of the data analysis and results. Since it is a longitudinal study, the mixed-methods approach provides an opportunity to devote individual attention to the semi-structured interview participants and diarists, yielding a very rich dataset and the opportunity to ask some of the same questions to a larger sample of individuals by way of a survey (White and Connaway, 2011–12; Connaway et al., 2013; Connaway et al., forthcoming).

A purposive convenience sample was selected that represents individuals from the four defined educational stages in the UK and the US and within specific disciplines and socio-economic levels. This was done in order to document behaviours as the participants make the transition between educational stages. The first educational stage, the Emerging stage, includes high school/secondary school seniors and first-year college/university students. The second stage, the Establishing stage, includes undergraduate students in their second through fourth years, while the third stage, the Embedding stage, includes postgraduate and doctoral students. The fourth stage, the Experiencing stage, includes faculty, scholars and researchers (Table 4.1).

Table 4.1 *Educational stages and number of participants in each stage*		
Educational stage	**Definition**	**Initial number of participants**
Emerging	Last-year high school/secondary school and first-year undergraduate college/university students	31 in the first group (15 UK, 16 US) 12 in the second group (6 UK, 6 US)
Establishing	Upper division undergraduate college/university students	10 (5 UK, 5 US)
Embedding	Postgraduate/graduate/doctoral students	10 (5 UK, 5 US)
Experiencing	Faculty/scholars/researchers	10 (5 UK, 5 US)

The first group of Emerging stage students, from 2011, was composed of 15 high school/secondary students and 16 first-year university students. Fifteen were from the UK and 16 from the US. Nineteen were female and twelve were male. Sixteen were between the ages of 12 and 18, eleven were between the ages of 19 and 25, while four were aged 26 years or older. In 2013, a second group of 12 Emerging stage participants were interviewed to establish a longitudinal comparison with the initial 31 Emerging stage participants. In the second group of Emerging students, six were high school/secondary students and six were first-year university students. Six were from the UK and six from the US. Five were female and seven were male. Nine were between the ages of 12 and 18 and three were between the ages of 19 and 25. A subset of five from this group also participated in monthly follow-up interviews or diary submissions over a six-month period during the spring and summer of 2013.

Semi-structured interviews

Semi-structured interviews were conducted with the 73 participants. Several of the interview questions utilized the critical incident technique, which asks individuals to recall specific incidences in which they experienced certain behaviours, actions and emotions (Flanagan, 1954; Connaway and Powell,

2010). This line of inquiry provided data about how and why they used and chose the sources, services and technologies during specific time periods and in specific instances. See the Appendix at the end of the case study for the semi-structured interview questions (p. 93).

The interviews lasted between 45 and 90 minutes and were conducted face to face, which provided an opportunity to ask questions and to probe for and elicit rich, detailed information about the participants' engagement with technology and how and why they got their information. The face-to-face interviews also provided opportunities for the research team to develop a rapport with the interviewees. This was important, since a subset of the interview participants were invited to continue to talk to the researchers or to submit diaries, on a monthly basis, for two and a half years (Connaway et al., forthcoming).

Diaries

Two subsets of interviewees (one group from all four of the educational stages of the first set of interviewees and one group from the second set of Emerging stage interviewees), comprising a total of 22 individuals, were selected to participate in the submission of monthly diaries during a two-and-a-half year period (from April 2011 to September 2013), after the initial face-to-face interview. A further four participants had been selected and volunteered to do diaries but then withdrew. The form for the diaries was left open-ended in order to get the most information from the participants and not to impose any preconceived assumptions onto their diary entries, since the researchers were not a part of the participants' everyday lives. The diarists were able to choose what they shared and how they shared their monthly diaries with the research team, i.e. instant messaging, text, e-mail, Skype, face to face, phone, video, etc. (Connaway et al., forthcoming; Somekh and Lewin, 2005; Wildemuth, 2009).

However, this open-ended strategy did not provide adequate information about how and why the participants engaged with services, systems and sources. Lists of websites with little explanation about why or how the sites had been accessed and used were submitted; thus, the diaries did not provide similarly rich datasets to those collected from the semi-structured interviews. Several of the diarists agreed to participate in monthly interviews and chose between Skype, face-to-face and phone for their discussions. See the Appendix for the monthly follow-up interview questions. A written version of the follow-up interviews was provided for those participants who preferred to document their monthly diaries. See the Appendix for the diary interview form. The follow-up interview questions and diary interview form included similar questions to those asked in the initial semi-structured interviews.

Online survey

In order to provide more context for the rich interview data gathered from our initial group of participants, an online survey was also a component of our project (White and Connaway, 2011–12). This survey provides a quantitative data-collection tool, and enables a multi-method approach for data comparison. Conducting a survey with a larger, non-probability, purposive, stratified sample enables the evaluation of the extent to which the results from the structured interviews and monthly diaries and discussions compare, and helps to determine whether the results from the smaller samples of qualitative data collection methods represent the broader population (Connaway and Powell, 2010). The survey was disseminated in December 2013 to 200 students and scholars (100 each from the US and UK, with 25 participants in each of the four educational stages) and is still underway at the time of writing.

The survey incorporates both open-ended critical-incident and multiple-choice questions. It includes some of the same questions asked in the first phases of the research project and others that were developed during the data-collection and analysis phases of the project. The survey takes approximately 30–45 minutes to complete. It was pre-tested and revised, based on the comments received, and pre-tested again before being disseminated to the study participants.

Findings

Comparison of first group of Emerging stage participants to second group of Emerging stage participants

When comparing the number of mentions of sources, decisions, motivations and contacts used by the first group of Emerging stage participants to the numbers for the second group of Emerging stage participants in interviews and diaries there is some difference. There are four notable differences between the participants of the two Emerging stage groups. Mentions are counted by the source (interview, diary or follow-up interview), meaning that the number of sources where the codes (coding is used to organize the data into segments that are then used to help with interpretation, and can allow the researcher to compare between different codes, for example how 'social' compares with 'private': see also Wikipedia: http://en.wikipedia.org/wiki/Qualitative_research) were found was divided by the total number of sources. The first is an increase of 31% in mentions of friends and colleagues as human sources (from 51%, n=40, N=78, in the first group to 83%, n=19, N=23, in the second group). Peers as human sources increased by 28% from 28% (n=22, N=78) in the first group to 57% (n=13, N=23) in the second group. There also is an increase of 30% in mentions of teachers and professors as human sources (from 44%, n=34, N=78, in the first group to 74%, n=17, N=23, in the second group). These increases in humans as sources may be attributed to an increased use of social media like Facebook, Skype, virtual learning environments, as well as communication via mobile phone. E-mail and texting are two of the top three choices of contact mentioned by both the first and second groups of Emerging stage participants. E-mail and texting are both mentioned by 45% (n=35, N=78) of the first group of participants, while e-mail is mentioned by 47% (n=11, N=23) and texting by 38% (n=9, N=23) of the second group of Emerging stage participants, with face-to-face coming in at 42% (n=10, N=23). Social networks are not just for connecting with friends and family but also for communicating with fellow students/classmates, peers, teachers/professors for assistance with coursework (Figure 4.1).

There is an increase from 13% (n=10, N=78) in the first group to 43% (n=10, N=23) in the second group for mentions of iPlayers and TV programmes. This reflects the general trend among students and the populace in general to turn to available online programming and media for entertainment, rather than to cable or television. This could be a result of the lower costs and more pervasive availability of iPlayers, mobile phones, tablets, etc. There is a 42% increase in mentions of the organization as the participants' motivation for using specific technologies (from 19% (n=15, N=78) in the first group to 61% (n=14, N=23) in the second group). This may reflect the increasing availability of scheduling tools to participants on their smartphones and other electronic devices.

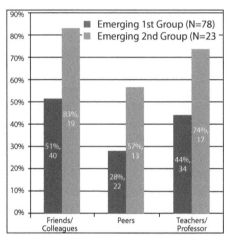

Figure 4.1 *Emerging groups and human sources*

Other differences include a 24% increase in mentions of e-books as digital sources (increasing from 24% (n=19, N=78) in the first group to 48% (n=11, N=23) in the second group), while the mentions of university databases increased by 5% (from 13% (n=10, N=78) in the first group to 17% (n=4, N=23) in the second group. An increase in e-book mentions may be related to a general increase in ownership of e-book readers and tablets. A recent Pew study showed that '50% of Americans now have a dedicated handheld device … for reading e-content' (Zickuhr and Rainie, 2014, 2). The increase in database mentions may not reflect an increase in usage. However, it does reflect the participants' awareness of the existence and/or availability of databases (Figure 4.2).

Convenience, as a means of decision or choice, is mentioned 28% more by the second group (63% (n=49, N=78) in the first group to 91% (n=21, N=23) in the second group). With more and more options available to students and faculty, the more convenient option will be considered and often be chosen. This supports the findings of Connaway, Dickey and Radford (2011), that convenience is the most important factor when selecting services and sources, and depends on the context and situation.

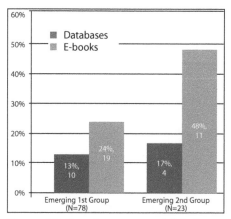

Figure 4.2 *Emerging groups and digital sources*

Comparison of the four educational stage participants

The analysis of the complete set of data indicates some differences between and similarities among the participants of the four educational stages. There is a steady increase of mentions of databases as a source, from 14% (n=14, N=101) by the Emerging stage to 21% (n=12, N=58) by the Establishing stage, then to 50% (n=8, N=16) by the Embedding stage, and ultimately to 76% (n=13, N=17) by the Experiencing stage. This may be attributed to an increased need in reliable, trustworthy and authoritative sources as individuals progress through their educational stages, which is exemplified by the high number of mentions of databases by faculty, scholars and researchers. It also could be that as one progresses through the educational phases, the term 'database' becomes more common (Figure 4.3).

There is an increase of mentions by the Embedding stage participants of authority/legitimacy, convenience and reliability as a means of deciding or choosing which sources to use. The mentions of authority/legitimacy increase from 51% (n=52, N=101) by the Emerging stage participants to 81% (n=13, N=16) by the Embedding stage participants. This may reflect the transition of graduate/postgraduate students to faculty, scholars and researchers within their disciplines. The mentions of currency of sources increase as well, from 9% (n=9, N=101) by the Emerging stage participants to 63% (n=10, N=16) by the Embedding stage participants. This may be related to graduate/postgraduate students' need to confirm that their dissertation or thesis research topic is unique and has not been studied previously, as well as the need to be aware of the most up-to-date research in their respective disciplines. Lastly, there is a rise in the consideration of reliability from 35% (n=35, N=101) at the Emerging stage to 63% (n=10, N=16) at the Embedding stage (Figure 4.4).

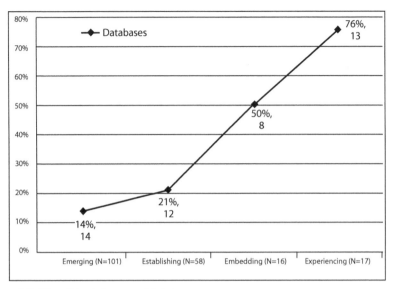

Figure 4.3 *Educational stages and databases*

Mentions of the decision to use e-mail as the means of contact for information sources increase in the later educational stages. The Emerging stage participants mention e-mail as a means of contact 52% of the time (n=53, N=101). The mention of e-mail increases to 66% (n=38, N=58) for the Establishing stage participants and continues to increase to 94% (n=15, N=16) for the Embedding stage participants. Mentions of e-mail by the Experiencing stage participants decrease slightly, to 88% (n=15, N=17). However, this still is a relatively high level of mentions when compared to those of the Emerging stage participants. This may indicate that e-mail becomes quite important for communication and as one progresses through academic life and as one becomes more accustomed to the academic community's methods of communication (Figure 4.5).

The mention of the use of face-to-face contact increases from 35% (n=35, N=101) by the Emerging stage participants to 40% (n=23, N=58) by the Establishing stage participants, and to 50% (n=8, N=16) by the Embedding stage participants, peaking at 76% (n=13, N=17) by the Experiencing stage participants. This indicates more face-to-face contact as one progresses through the educational stages. This may be attributed to occasions that faculty and researchers may encounter, such as impromptu 'water cooler' conversations or meetings with students, or the increased opportunities when attending conferences and meetings, etc.

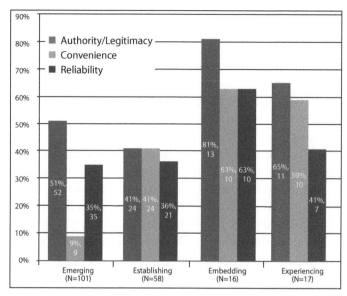

Figure 4.4 *Educational stages and decision*

Implications for library services and systems, and conclusions

'Access to information is ubiquitous and information permeates all aspects of our lives' (Moran and Marchionini, 2012, 97). In the past, the library was one of the only sources available for obtaining information; thus, users built their

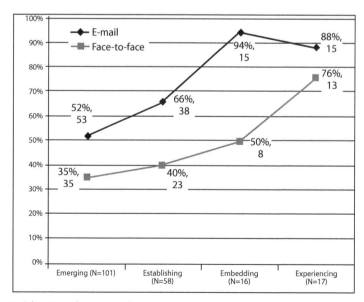

Figure 4.5 *Educational stages and contact*

workflows around the library because they had more attention time to give to the search. However, in the current information environment information resources are prevalent, but users do not have extra time (or will not make extra time) to search for information or to learn about a new source, discovery service, or access methods (Dempsey, 2008). This implies that library services need to be geared towards individuals' work environments and convenience. The sources need to be easy to discover, access and use, and the technologies need to be easy to use.

The results from the V&R project indicate that databases are still a part of the academic culture and are authoritative, convenient and trustworthy sources. In order to make databases more easily discoverable and accessible through web browsers, librarians need to make users aware that they are available. Databases should be promoted in both the physical and virtual libraries and in face-to-face and virtual communications with users, especially with secondary/high school and undergraduate students, as well as in social networks. Also, the inclusion of links to library sources such as databases in Wikipedia will make them readily and conveniently available.

The increased mention of e-books from the first group of secondary/high school students and undergraduate students to the second group indicates greater awareness of them, which may be attributed to ease of accessibility by downloading, and to the ownership of devices that are e-book ready. This is an opportunity for librarians to advertise e-book offerings and to make them increasingly available.

In light of the increasing number of students using social media, namely Facebook, to connect with fellow students for homework help, providing easy access to librarian reference (or other homework help sites from Facebook or other social media outlets) could prove helpful to students and an opportunity for librarians to connect with students in the event that peer help fails. The availability of virtual reference services (VRS) as pop-up chat help on library websites or via web searches or social question-and-answer sites are ways for libraries to market the VRS service.

Overall, the library experience needs to be more like the experience currently available on the open web (e.g. Wikipedia, Google, Amazon.com, iTunes) (Connaway, Dickey and Radford, 2011). The mention of iPads and TV programmes increased from the first group of secondary/high school students and undergraduate students to the second group. With that in mind, this may be an opportune time to promote the availability of apps and programs for iPlayers, e-books, blogs and open-source materials via the library. Another way to embed library services into individual workflows is to offer and promote access to digital media such as documentaries, movies and television shows through Hoopla and other services.

Considering that the mentions of face-to-face communication increased as participants progressed through educational stages, this is still an important aspect of contact within all the educational stages. Library staff should be prominently visible and approachable in campus libraries, social areas and classes. Also, e-mail use is still prevalent among the participants in all of the educational stages. Therefore, it would be beneficial to promote librarian e-mail contacts and VRS. Relationship building in both face-to-face and virtual environments continues to be a critical factor in information seeking (Connaway and Radford, 2011).

This sample of the V&R project results provides an example of rich data that can be garnered by utilizing mixed-methods research, qualitative research methods and data-collection tools. Gathering qualitative data directly from users can help to identify the challenges they experience when using and accessing library services and systems, and also opportunities for the development of new services and systems that better meet their individual needs. A mixed method of inquiry can be used to measure the effectiveness of library services and systems and to articulate the value and impact of libraries on the academic community.

Appendix: Case Study 4.1 methods

We conducted immersive observations and structured interviews and also solicited photo diaries. The interview data, combined with the photos that students took of their everyday academic environments, provided a rich picture of the ways in which they did and did not engage with institutional higher education spaces like libraries.

Some of the interview questions (especially the 'magic wand' question) have been asked in very much the same way of a variety of researchers since the year 2000.[1]

Structured interview questions

1   *Describe the things you enjoy doing with technology and the web each week.*
    This is a conversational start in order to put the interviewees at their
    ease. We are trying to get a sense of their overall digital literacy so that
    we can set their information-seeking behaviours within a broader
    context. Do they socialize online? (See probe.) Do they 'contribute'
    online in the form of pictures, video, blogs, etc.?
    [PROBES: How important is the web for your social life, do you use it to
    keep in touch with your friends? What gadgets/devices/things do you
    use the most, is there anything you 'couldn't live without'? How much
    time on average do you spend online each week? Is there anything that
    bothers you about being online?]

2   *Think of the ways you have used technology and the web for your studies. Describe a typical week.*
We are looking at interviewees' use of educational technologies more specifically for study. We hope they will start to introduce informal learning, self-directed study, peer-to-peer learning, etc. We anticipate that they will (or may not) mention Facebook, MySpace, etc. [PROBES: How do you keep track of things? What systems for learning online do you have? Can you give us any examples of when you've asked your friends for help on assignments/homework online? What kinds of online resources have you found that help you with your studies? How did you find them? What other gadgets or devices do you use for your studies?]

3   *What did you think university studies would be like when you were in high school? How is your experience different from what you thought it would be? Describe what you think the next stage of your education will be. Tell me what you think this will be like.*
[PROBES: How do you think you will use technology in the next part of your education? If you think you will need to adapt the way you use technology, what sort of changes do you think you'll make?]

4   *When starting an assignment (e.g. an assessed essay for a coursework deadline) what is the first thing that you do?*
[PROBE: Do you: select a question that you already feel confident about; check your lecture notes to see if they help answer the question; check out what your friends are doing; surf the web to see if it has some suitable material; read one of the assigned readings?]

5   *When preparing an essay, where do you primarily get the information: your notes from a lecture; recommended readings; information on the web; information from fellow students; personal experience on fieldwork, etc.?*
[PROBE: Are there any of these that you feel you would never use to answer an essay question? Why not?]

6   *Think of a time when you had a situation where you needed information and you did a quick search and made do with it. You knew there were other sources but you decided not to use them. Please include sources such as friends, family, professors, teaching assistants, tutors, coaches, etc. Prompt for both academic and informal (domestic, personal …) examples.*
[PROBES: Did you simply take the first answer/solution you were able to find? What was the situation? What sources did you use? What led you to use them … and not others? Did they help? How? What sources

did you decide not to use? What led to this/these decision/s? What did source A give you that you thought source B could not? Are there situations where source B would be a better choice for you? How did you decide when it was time to stop looking? How did you assess what was good enough?]

7   *Have there been times when you were told to use recommended readings from the library or virtual learning environment and used other source(s) instead?* [PROBE: What made you decide not to use what you were asked to use? What kinds of things do your instructors want you to do when you're looking for information? Does what you do look like that, and if not, what does it look like?]

8   *If you had a magic wand, what would your ideal way of getting information be? How would you go about using the systems and services? When? Where? How?*

9   *What comments or questions do you have for me? Is there anything you would like me to explain? What would you like to tell me that you've thought about during this interview?*

Photo diaries prompts

The photo diaries were requested from UNC students with the intention of getting the students to document what their academic and personal spaces are like, in a situation where the anthropologist did not have the time or resources to follow the students home. This instrument is adapted from similar ones used in the ERIAL project (www.erialproject.org):

1   The place you most often use in the library
2   The computer you use in the library, showing its surroundings
3   Your favourite place to study
4   The place where you keep your books
5   Your communication devices (e.g. phone, laptop, tablet)
6   The location where you most frequently use your computer (if you have one)
7   The best place for writing a paper
8   Something you can't live without
9   Your commute to campus
10 Your most difficult course this semester
11 Your favourite part of the day
12 The night before a big assignment is due

13 Something that makes you laugh
14 All the stuff you take to campus to do research
15 The most helpful person/thing in the library
16 Something you've noticed that you think others don't notice
17 How you manage your time or keep track of your work
18 The tools you use for writing assignments
19 Your favourite person(s) to study with
20 Your favourite archaeological site, artefact or person
21 Your least favourite archaeological site, artefact or person
22 Your fieldwork notebook
23 Images of the screen of a computer you are using, showing research documents
24 A place in the library where you feel lost
25 Images of open books as (if) used in your research
26 Something really weird
27 Images of drafts
28 Your least favourite place in the library
29 Whatever you want

CASE STUDY 4.2

Ethnographic techniques and new visions for libraries

Donna Lanclos (University of North Carolina, Charlotte)

Introduction

Pierre Bourdieu's 1965 ethnography of French undergraduate university student behaviour, *Academic Discourse*, includes an essay entitled 'The Users of Lille University Library' (co-authored with Monique de Saint Martin). The concerns expressed about undergraduate academic behaviour appear to have changed not at all, not after the passage of over 40 years, and not in the transition from French academia to that of the US and UK. Bourdieu worries about their lack of attention to librarians: 'Students reject working through a librarian, rarely asking for assistance. "It is very difficult," a librarian says; "there is a door to go through, they don't know, they dare not"' (Bourdieu, 1994, 132).

Bourdieu says that students don't work in the library because it does not suit their needs: 'Students in their great majority do nothing at the Library which they cannot do as well or better at home because, by unanimous consent, the Library is an unfavourable site for scholarly reflection' (Bourdieu, 1994, 123). He goes on to say that 'most users of the Library only appear to be working rather than actually getting anything done' (p. 123). The work of academia that Bourdieu clearly hoped to see in the Library (reading, thinking) was actually, according to students, being done in spaces such as cafés, bedrooms, even on walks, 'in circumstances where other, non-studious activities can be fit in' (p. 124).

In short, Bourdieu was confronted with students who were uncomfortable working in the library, who preferred to do their academic work where they were comfortable. The students went to the library if their professors insisted (frequently to check out or refer to a book). Their presence in the library had as much social as academic purpose. On the face of it, academic libraries are still grappling with much the same issues as Bourdieu and his colleagues described in the mid-1960s.

Qualitative research – in-depth research focused on understanding human behaviour – can illuminate the details and logic behind decisions that are only partially revealed by the relatively limited, prescriptive questions asked by large-scale surveys. The writing of deeply observed pictures of human behaviour is called ethnography (literally, 'writing culture'), and is an approach that originates in anthropology. Conducting ethnographic work in higher education can facilitate a better understanding of the learning habits of students and serve to evaluate the effectiveness of learning spaces such as libraries, classrooms and less conventional places. Such an understanding can also lead to future developments in this area and help to target better support for the students' needs.

As the roles of technology, place and culture shift, they also transform the everyday practices of people who need to find, use and produce scholarship, whether in books, journals, websites or manuscripts. There is at this time an increasing amount of research conducted on university campuses among undergraduates and faculty, undertaken to inform libraries and information scientists about the behaviours individuals engage in during their conduct of academic work, inside and out of academic environments (see, for example, Asher and Duke, 2011; Connaway, Dickey and Radford, 2011; Delcore, Mullooly and Scroggins, 2009; Foster and Gibbons, 2007; Gabridge, Gaskell, and Stout, 2008; Head and Eisenberg, 2009). My work at UNC Charlotte (Wu and Lanclos, 2011) with Jisc/OCLC (for example: www.jisc.ac.uk/whatwedo/ projects/visitorsandresidents.aspx), and in collaboration with University College London (Lanclos and Gourlay, 2014) has been directed at trying to understand the ways in which people in a variety of different educational stages conceive of and use academic spaces such as university libraries. Common to all of these projects is reliance on a suite of methodological approaches, including photo diaries, structured interviews and immersive/participant observation.

In the following case study I describe the work I have done at UNC Charlotte, to illustrate the ways in which such qualitative research can inform policies around space, services and the role of academic libraries in higher education.

UNC Charlotte: collaborative spaces for students

Since my arrival at Atkins Library in 2009 I have been consistently paying attention to what students are trying to do during their academic work, throughout the Library and elsewhere on campus. Students were observed trying to work in pairs or threes at traditional library carrels, we noted how overbooked our group study rooms were, we saw the syllabi requiring that students work in groups as a part of their coursework. Photo-diary data collected from UNC Charlotte undergraduates revealed the wide range of non-library spaces in which the students did their academic work, as well as the lack of a variety of such spaces in the Library.

It became clear that the Library needed to gather additional on-site data that would allow for an argument for the construction of purpose-built collaborative work spaces in the library.

Three different graduate students served as my research assistants in 2012 and 2013 (Mitch McGregor and Allison Schaefer in the Department of Architecture, and Carrie Vass in the Department of Communications), contributing their drafting expertise as well as giving time and effort to immersive observation, after first being trained by me in ethnographic techniques. The first graduate student worked on the ground floor prior to its renovation, when we were still thinking about how to create collaborative work spaces (McGregor, 2012). After observations and a few low-technology experiments in different parts of the Library, we chose the corridor on the Atkins ground floor connecting the main stairs and the coffee shop as the area of study. This space had areas that allowed both private and group work, mainly due to the type of furniture and its arrangement (Figure 4.6).

During observations in the Library we sketched diagrams to illustrate the types of activities that were taking place in the spaces. Figures 4.7 to 4.9 show some examples (all sketches created in Adobe Illustrator by McGregor).

Figure 4.7 shows the long table that tended to attract students studying alone on the left. The 'living room' arrangement is in the centre, comprising a couch, chairs and coffee and end-tables. In this sketch, two students are working at the white-board and using the coffee table to hold the laptop and the textbook they are consulting for their studies.

Figure 4.6
Part of the ground floor in Atkins Library, Spring 2012 (photo by M. McGregor)

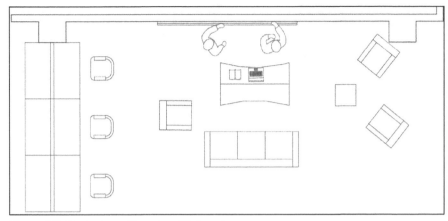

Figure 4.7 *Students working at a whiteboard*

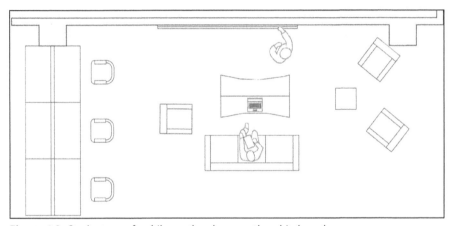

Figure 4.8 *Student on sofa while another draws on the whiteboard*

In Figure 4.8 one student is taking notes on the couch, referring to material on the laptop, while the other sketches out thoughts on the whiteboard.

In Figure 4.9 the student at the long table is referring to a textbook and laptop while the other uses the whiteboard to think through the reference materials.

Our goal in conducting these observations was to understand what people were coming to this space to do and, rather than recreate the space with a new type of activity in mind, to redesign the space so as to enhance its current use. Student groups would come to the space to work on problems or to brainstorm, often using the whiteboard while referring to a book or laptop. This was often difficult because there was no place to put books or laptops that was adjacent to the whiteboard. Other groups used the space to work on group presentations, sitting in the couch area and working from one or

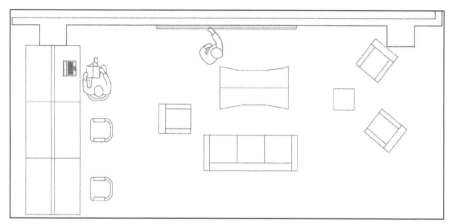

Figure 4.9 *Student referring to textbook while another uses the whiteboard*

multiple laptops, discussing a group project. There was a clear need for:

• screens
• whiteboards
• configurable furniture
• flexible notions of group size and possible activities.

We designed an intervention that would provide a large screen adjacent to the whiteboard that students could hook up to their laptops. To allow for multiple uses, the screen could be connected to while one was working near the whiteboard, as well from the sitting area facing the screen (Figure 4.10).

Once the screen was set up, we spent about 56 hours observing this space in a single week, varying the time of observations from early morning to after midnight. The screen station was used for everything from a cell phone-charging station, to practising PowerPoint presentations, to solving physics equations. We conducted several interviews and asked users of different varieties what they liked and disliked about the space

Figure 4.10 *Whiteboard and large computer screen near the sitting area (Photo by M. McGregor)*

and what could be improved. Most students said they really liked how they could move things around in the space, such as the furniture, or where they connected to the screen. The space met their basic needs and was adaptable to the needs of specific groups. The more flexible spaces can be, the more apt people are to use them (Figure 4.11).

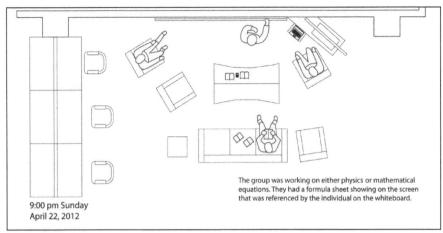

The group was working on either physics or mathematical equations. They had a formula sheet showing on the screen that was referenced by the individual on the whiteboard.

9:00 pm Sunday
April 22, 2012

Figure 4.11 *Flexible study space being used by students (Sketch by M. McGregor)*

Students wanted a semi-private space that they could adapt for various types of group work. The possibility of having multiple types of media showing information at the same time, in this case whiteboard and media screen, allows groups to function even more efficiently. Students also want this technology to be easy to use; if the technology in this space requires too much effort to learn, it is possible that students will avoid it.

While this qualitative data was just part of the information we compiled and responded to in thinking about and designing the new ground floor, it was a crucial part. It allowed us not just to document the demand for such spaces, but to be specific about what the content (in terms of furniture types and technology) of the space should be. Because it was grounded in the actual behaviour of our students, we could use this work to think through ahead of time the details that demanded our attention. Overall, a research-based process allows designers and educators to greatly increase the possibility of creating successful spaces.

Space previously used by library staff has now been renovated and transformed into an array of spaces in which students can undertake collaborative work (Figures 4.12 to 4.15, photos by Cheryl Lansford, Interior Designer for UNC Charlotte).

There are configurable furniture arrangements in some areas, and more fixed arrangements in others. Figure 4.12 shows touch-screen tables which also have screens at the head of the table, so students can plug in and share from their laptops.

Figure 4.13 is a view into one of our new group study rooms, with wheeled tables as well as wheeled task chairs. Surfaces near the digital screens allow students to share from their laptops, and there is also a dedicated computer for them to work from if they do not have their own device with them.

Figure 4.12 *Touch-screen tables*

Figure 4.13 *Group study rooms*

Whiteboards and the glass walls are meant to be written on (and are).

The space just outside of the library café (Figure 4.14) has been set up with predominantly café-type seating, but with larger low tables so as to accommodate groups' need to spread out their laptops, books, notebooks and other 'stuff' that they are working with. There are power outlets in the

Figure 4.14 *Café-style seating space outside the library café*

Figure 4.15 *Highly configurable space*

wood-panelled pillars to allow students to plug in their equipment/devices wherever they want to work.

The most configurable part of the open space, the space not contained in the study rooms (Figure 4.15), has more of the wheeled tables and task chairs, as well as some soft seating (relatively lightweight, so it can be moved around), rolling whiteboards and movable privacy screens.

Space assessment

In many learning-space design scenarios, the opening is the end. Universities continue to build new spaces, open them and then walk away without thinking about what comes next. What did they get right about the new spaces? What did we get wrong? How can we improve it? When can we make changes? At UNC Charlotte, we immediately began qualitative research into the uses of our new ground-floor spaces, to better respond to how people were actually using the space, rather than assuming that they were using the space as we imagined they would.

After the grand opening of the new Atkins Library ground-floor collaborative study commons in January 2013, we observed and mapped activities within the space (Schaefer, 2013).

Over the course of our observations we mapped the kinds of activities people were doing, and also where people walked when they moved through the space. We then generated several activity maps (all maps created by Allison Schaefer).

Figure 4.16 shows where people were eating during Allison's observations (about 8 hours altogether). The heavily shaded areas are adjacent to the library café. But eating is clearly happening near the nice windows overlooking the

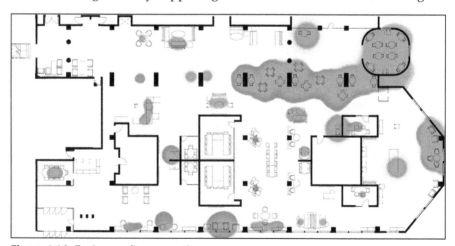

Figure 4.16 *Zoning use diagram: eating zones*

Student Activity centre (on the right in this diagram) and in the central parts of the spaces.

Figure 4.17 shows that studying is happening throughout the space, in high-traffic areas as well as quiet, isolated parts of the floor.

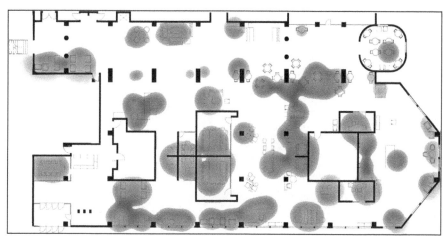

Figure 4.17 *Zoning use diagram: study zones*

Figure 4.18 shows that talking is also happening throughout the ground-floor space, with a few exceptions.

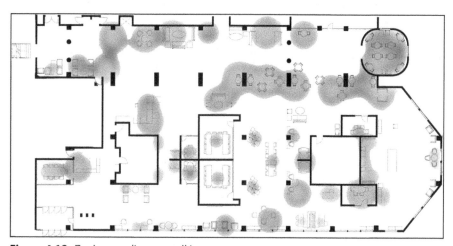

Figure 4.18 *Zoning use diagram: talking zones*

When we overlap the maps for eating and studying (Figure 4.19), we see that these are not mutually exclusive areas. These maps were created from afternoon observations – if they had included evening hours, we know that there would have been even more overlap. Atkins Library has allowed food and drink in its spaces (except in Special Collections) for several years now, and Figure 4.19 shows that we are right to not treat these activities (eating and studying) as mutually exclusive.

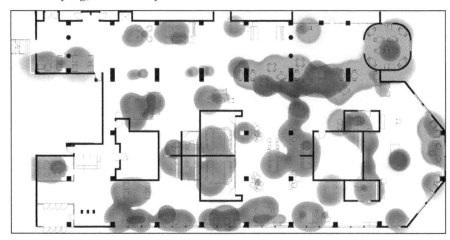

Figure 4.19 *Zoning use diagram: eating and studying zones*

Students study and talk at the same time (Figure 4.20). While some areas clearly show one thing or the other happening, the overlap is significant.

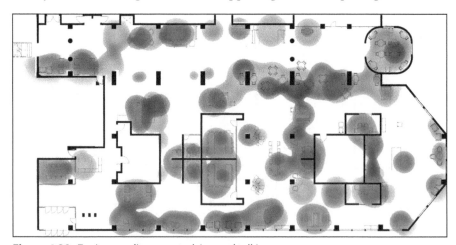

Figure 4.20 *Zoning use diagram: studying and talking zones*

Just because students have a laptop open does not mean that they are studying. Likewise, just because they don't have a laptop doesn't mean they are not studying (Figure 4.21).

While our observations revealed our success in creating a space for students that could accommodate a wide range of activities, and in providing furniture

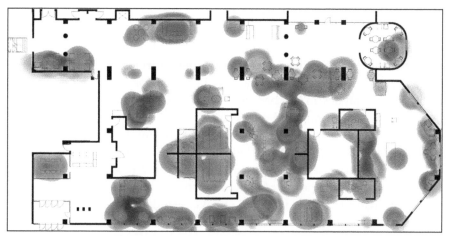

Figure 4.21 *Zoning use diagram: studying and laptop zones*

and technology that could support and encourage those activities, we also discovered some things that need to be fixed. We added a service point to the area near the North Entrance, to accommodate student needs for checking out and returning library materials, as well as asking directional questions. We discovered that there was not enough furniture in all of the parts of the space, so we have moved in more soft seating and more rolling tables. The tall café tables were too small to accommodate student 'spreading out,' so we have added more tables so they can be pulled together to create more work space. We are continuing to observe and think about the use of touch-screen technology in the space, as it is still unclear how the affordances of touch screens fit with the academic computational needs of our patrons.

Conclusions

One advantage to having a full-time ethnographer on the Library's staff is that part of the value of an ethnographic approach is the possibility to be embedded in the environment over long periods of time. Short-term contract work or grant-funded research that lasts only a few years is better than nothing, but longitudinal research that is fully integrated into the everyday workings of the library allows the best chance to respond in an agile way to conditions 'on the ground'.

Integrating a qualitative-data agenda into the analytics that libraries rely on to inform policies about space and services can involve actually hiring a full-time ethnographer. It remains to be seen in the US whether this model will proliferate (there are currently only two anthropologists working full time as ethnographers in US academic libraries, as of this writing). The

London School of Economics hired a library ethnographer in 2014, inspired by the potential for library ethnography. My own experience of working with graduate student researchers demonstrates that engaging our own students on campus in a research role can be a valuable contribution, too.

Higher education, and thus academic libraries, has historically relied on quantitative analytics, in part because of a policy orientation where evaluation is equivalent to counting and measuring (as with grading assignments, for example). But assessment should be about the information that can be gathered to inform changes and, ideally, improvements. Qualitative data gathering like that which occurs in ethnographic research can provide valuable insights into the logic behind the actions of the people whom higher education institutions are trying to engage – students as well as academic staff. As is shown in this case study, such insights can be constructively used to make arguments for improvements and changes. Crafting policy is about constructing a compelling narrative, and qualitative analytics such as ethnographic data are tailor made for the grounded storytelling in which libraries and other parts of higher education need to engage so as to draw resources and attention to their value.

Chapter conclusion

The case studies described in this chapter demonstrate the importance of going beyond the quantitative data that is so often the focus of analytics and data-driven decision making in institutions and organizations. By itself this analytics data provides only a part of the overall story. Analytics data is very effective for telling you *what* your users are doing, and quite possibly *how* they are doing it. But what it cannot tell you is *why* they are doing it.

It is the 'why' which also opens up the possibility of identifying new potential services and interventions that can meet undeclared user needs and transform the experience for users. More fundamentally, the ethnographic and mixed-methods approaches described in this chapter place the user at the heart of developments. The user (data) – rather than any departmental or administrative requirement – is effectively driving decision making.

In the next chapter we begin to explore how we can further place the user at the centre of the services and collections that we deliver by understanding the use of and interactions across the web. We will begin to track the user beyond both the virtual and physical confines of the library, out into the open web.

Qualitative library research: further resources

If you'd like to find out more about the work described in this chapter, and access further reading and inspiration, below are additional resources for individuals and institutions interested in qualitative methodologies for libraries and cultural heritage organizations more generally.

More on the case studies
- Evaluating Digital Services: A Visitors and Residents Approach, www.jiscinfonet.ac.uk/infokits/evaluating-services.
- Anthropology in the Stacks blog, http://atkinsanthro.blogspot.co.uk.

Additional resources
- Ethnography, Usability and User Experience in Libraries (blog), http://ukanthrolib.wordpress.com.
- Journal of Library User Experience, http://weaveux.org.
- Ethnographic Research in Illinois Academic Libraries (ERIAL), www.erialproject.org.

Note
1   According to Dr Lynn Connaway at OCLC (personal communication, February 2012): 'We used the questions first on the Sense-making study and then Seeking Synchronicity. The project URLs are below:

Institute for Museums and Library Services Research Grant, 2003–05. "Sense-making the Information Confluence: The Hows and the Whys of College and University User Satisficing of Information Needs," Brenda Dervin, Ohio State University, Principal Investigator; Lynn Silipigni Connaway and Chandra Prabha, OCLC Research, Co-Investigators. Project Website URL: www.oclc.org/research/activities/past/orprojects/imls/default.htm.

Institute for Museums and Library Services Research Grant, 2005–07. "Seeking Synchronicity: Evaluating Virtual Reference Services from User, Non-User, and Librarian Perspectives." Lynn Silipigni Connaway, OCLC Research, and Marie L. Radford, Rutgers University, Co-Principal Investigators. Project Website URL: www.oclc.org/research/activities/synchronicity/default.htm.

We also used them in the current WorldCat.org study – www.oclc.org/research/activities/recommender/default.htm. We're analyzing the data now.'

References
Case Study 4.1
Connaway, L. S. (forthcoming) Why Libraries? A call for user-centered assessment, *Textos Universitaris de Biblioteconomia i Documentacio*.

Connaway, L. S. and Powell, R. R. (2010) *Basic Research Methods for Librarians*, Libraries Unlimited.

Connaway, L. S. and Radford, M. L. (2011) *Seeking Synchronicity: revelations and recommendations for virtual reference*, OCLC Research, www.oclc.org/reports/synchronicity/full.pdf.

Connaway, L. S. and Radford, M. L. (2013) *Academic Library Assessment: beyond the basics.* Presented at Raynor Memorial Libraries, Marquette University, 18 July, Milwaukee, Wisconsin.

Connaway, L. S., Dickey, T. J. and Radford, M. L. (2011) 'If It Is too Inconvenient I'm not Going after It:' convenience as a critical factor in information-seeking behaviors, *Library and Information Science Research*, **33** (3), 179–90.

Connaway, L. S., Lanclos, D. M. and Hood, E. M. (2013) 'I Always Stick with the First Thing that Comes up on Google …': where people go for information, what they use, and why, *EDUCAUSE Review Online*, 6 December, www.educause.edu/ero/article/i-always-stick-first-thing-comes-google-where-people-go-information-what-they-use-and-why.

Connaway, L. S., White, D., Lanclos, D. and Hood, E. M. (forthcoming) *Visitors and Residents Library Evaluation Infokit.*

Connaway, L. S., Lanclos, D., White, D., Le Cornu, A. and Hood, E. M. (2013) User-centered Decision Making: a new model for developing academic library services and systems, *IFLA Journal*, **39** (1), 30–6.

Dempsey, L. (2008) Always On: libraries in a world of permanent connectivity, *First Monday*, **14** (1), http://firstmonday.org/article/view/2291/2070.

Flanagan, J. C. (1954) The Critical Incident Technique, *Psychological Bulletin*, **51** (4), 327–58.

Glazier, J. D. and Powell, R. R. (eds) (1992) *Qualitative Research in Information Management*, Libraries Unlimited.

Kaufman, P. and Watstein, S. B. (2008) Library Value (Return on Investment, ROI) and the Challenge of Placing a Value on Public Services, *Reference Services Review*, **36**, 226–31.

Moran, B. and Marchionini, G. (2012) Information Professionals 2050: educating the next generation of information professionals, *Information Services and Use*, **32** (3/4), 95–100.

Somekh, B. and Lewin, C. (2005) *Research Methods in the Social Sciences*, Sage.

White, D. S. and Connaway, L. S. (2011–12) *Visitors and Residents: what motivates engagement with the digital information environment?* Funded by Jisc, OCLC and Oxford University, www.oclc.org/research/activities/vandr/ and www.jisc.ac.uk/whatwedo/projects/visitorsandresidents.aspx.

Wildemuth, B. M. (2009) *Applications of Social Research Methods to Questions in Information and Library Science,* Libraries Unlimited.

Zickuhr, K. and Rainie, L. (2014) *E-reading Rises as Device Ownership Jumps: three in ten adults read an e-book last year; half own a tablet or e-reader*, Pew Research Center, www.pewinternet.org/files/2014/01/PIP_E-reading_011614.pdf.

Case Study 4.2

Asher, A. D. and Duke, L. M. (2011) *College Libraries and Student Culture: what we now know*, American Library Association.

Bourdieu, P. (1994) *Academic Discourse: linguistic misunderstanding and professorial power*, Stanford University Press.

Connaway, L. S., Dickey, T. J. and Radford, M. L. (2011) 'If It is too Inconvenient I'm not Going after It': convenience as a critical factor in information-seeking behaviors, *Library and Information Science Research*, **33** (3), 179–90.

Delcore, H. D., Mullooly, J. and Scroggins, M. (2009) *The Library Study at Fresno State*, Institute of Public Anthropology, California State University, Fresno, CA, www.csufresno.edu/anthropology/ipa/TheLibraryStudy%28DelcoreMullooly Scroggins%29.pdf.

Foster, N. F. and Gibbons, S. (2007) *Studying students: the Undergraduate Research Project at the University of Rochester*, Association of College and Research Libraries.

Gabridge, T., Gaskell, M. and Stout, A. (2008) Information Seeking through Students' Eyes: the MIT Photo Diary Study, *College and Research Libraries*, November, 510–22.

Head, A. J. and Eisenberg, M. B. (2009) *Lessons Learned: how college students seek information in the digital age*, Project Information Literacy First Year Report with Student Survey Findings, University of Washington's Information School, 1 December.

Lanclos, D. and Gourlay, L. (2014) The Intersection of the Digital and Material Practices in Contemporary Library Spaces. SRHE seminar, *The Digital and the Material: mapping contemporary student practices*, School of Research in Higher Education, 28 March, London, UK.

McGregor, M. L. (2012) Principles of Space and Interaction, unpublished MA thesis, Department of Architecture, University of North Carolina, Charlotte, NC.

Schaefer, A. (2013) *Interactive Design: an exchange of social awareness, sense, and substance*, unpublished MA thesis, Department of Architecture, University of North Carolina, Charlotte, NC.

Wu, S. K. and Lanclos, D. (2011) Re-imagining the Users' Experience: an ethnographic approach to web usability and space design, *Reference Services Review*, **39** (3), 369–89.

Web and social media metrics for the cultural heritage sector

Chapter overview

We have, until now, largely stayed within both the physical and virtual confines of the library, archive or institution as we have explored how analytics and metrics can improve services and help to support decision making. However, it is now time to step outside the boundaries of the institution and look at analytics and metrics in relation to the open web; in particular, to explore examples and approaches for cultural heritage institutions using web analytics and metrics to help drive and improve impact and user engagement on the web.

This chapter provides two case studies which present a picture of how some of the UK's biggest and most popular cultural heritage organizations (like the British Museum, British Library, Tate Gallery, V&A [Victoria and Albert Museum] and Wellcome Collection) take advantage of web metrics and analytics. The case studies provide unique insights, tips and examples of how institutions are utilizing web metrics to better understand their users' behaviours, to improve their web and digital presences and to ensure maximum impact for what they are doing on the web. The two case studies in this chapter are:

- CASE STUDY 5.1 Stuart, D., *The web impact of cultural heritage institutions*, p. 117
- CASE STUDY 5.2 Malde, S. et al., *Let's Get Real: a Journey Towards Understanding and Measuring Digital Engagement*, p. 136.

Before we explore our case study examples it is worth dwelling on two new terms that this chapter has introduced – web metrics and social media metrics – and considering further why the web has become such a critical part of the work of the cultural heritage institution.

Web metrics and analytics in the cultural heritage sector

The Wikipedia entry for Web Analytics defines web metrics and analytics as 'the measurement, collection, analysis and reporting of web data for purposes of understanding and optimizing web usage'. As libraries, archives, galleries and museums direct greater focus and resources to the development of their online presence, so it becomes increasingly critical to capture and analyse users' online interactions and experiences. Like the institution's physical building, its web presence represents a vital part of an institution's existence.

The web is now the starting point for much of what we do: finding a painting via Google search, locating an article through a link in a blog post and so on. These online interactions often lead us to the collection or item in which we are interested on the institution's website, but we may not go beyond the Wikipedia page for an object, or even the Google search results page. It's crucial for cultural heritage institutions to find ways to ensure that their collections and content are available in the online spaces and places that people are already inhabiting on the web; for the institution, as it were, to go where people already are.

This means that there must be a shift in the kinds of online interactions cultural institutions are willing to have with their 'visitors'. They need to learn about the changing behaviours and expectations of users and visitors, and to discover not only how they interact with the institutional web pages, but where they have come from, where they go and how they engage with the web more generally. The web has become the location for our searching, discovery, use and even creation of content; it has transformed our expectations of what content and services should be like. It is thus essential for cultural institutions to understand the changing requirements and expectations of users, and they can do this by studying what their users are doing and where they are going on the web.

Add to this the fact that the institutional web presence may no longer be a single, discrete location, but may reflect the more complex range of social spaces that users occupy across the web. The institutional web presence is now likely to be complex, dynamic and multi-faceted. Its foundation is likely to be a website, but it may be accompanied by a range of other presences, from blogs and social media through to multimedia channels. Indeed, these community and social presences are fast becoming critical components in an institution's digital existence and in its interaction, engagement and communication with its network of users and visitors.

The social web

The web is a social engine – it drives social interactions and networks. As Sir Tim Berners-Lee has written: 'The Web is more a social creation than a technical one. I designed it for a social effect – to help people work together – and not as a technical toy' (Porter, 2008). The evolution of the web saw early development focused on the one-way communication of static web pages. However, further developments quickly began to enable two-way conversations and interactions, and eventually the emergence of 'social software' (Shirky, 2003) such as Wikipedia, where the affordances of the software are focused on the 'group', rather than the individual.

Of course, now the social web (and social software) is a ubiquitous and essential part of our web experience, from blogs and twitter to Facebook and YouTube. Cultural heritage institutions can no longer count on a single web presence, but instead need to inhabit multiple web spaces and, critically, engage with those spaces and the people in them in more meaningful ways. In fact, we might argue that the social web demands that institutions should behave as residents of the web, not merely visitors (White and Le Cornu, 2011). With a resident approach, the institution inhabits a digital space in much the same way that you might inhabit a physical space – you see yourself as part of that community, you converse and engage and effectively live part of your life or existence in that space. Part of you continues to exist when you are not online – your persona does not disappear, as it were, when you log off. This behaviour also means that we increasingly leave a trail – a 'data exhaust' – as we move across the web and interact with different spaces and networks.

The social web encourages the types of activities and interactions that produce large volumes of data – think about the number of tweets or Likes produced in one day, globally. Getting the data is, in some ways, not the problem. Rather, the problem is what we want to measure and why. In describing the challenges of measuring impact in journalism, Jonathan Stray articulates the challenge of abundant data:

> We are awash in metrics, and we have the ability to engage with readers at scale in ways that would have been impossible (or impossibly expensive) in an analog world. The problem now is figuring out which data to pay attention to and which to ignore.

(Stray, 2012)

In this chapter we are primarily interested in how web metrics can shed light on a cultural heritage institution's impact and engagement on the web. For metrics on impact and engagement there will be the largely numerical data related to page hits, views, Likes and so forth. These are what we might describe as classic web metrics – the data telling us what people are doing, where and how often. In terms of engagement we might also be interested in how many new people visited a website, or how many left a comment or shared a story or piece of content, for example.

These numbers are important. They enable us to compare our own institution to other institutions in a standard way, to track our progress and to uncover new insights into our audiences and content. But impact and engagement have much deeper aspects, which institutions could and should be measuring. For example: what is the wider impact of a piece of content? How did it change or influence something – such as government policy? Why does someone likes a particular blog post? – How did it improve their learning experience? Questions such as these begin to challenge and question the assumptions that underpin our current approach to web metrics. Why do we want more people to share our content? Is the size of the audience important, or do we want to get the content in front of specific audiences or people? Increasingly the web is allowing us to consider the 'bigger' metrics that can uncover the implications for us, as institutions, of our impact and engagement, and the breadth and depth of data generated through the social web challenge us to consider concepts such as engagement and impact in more nuanced ways.

While much of our attention is still directed to collecting and analysing the more traditional types of metrics, cultural institutions are increasingly recognizing that the web metrics of the future may look somewhat different to what we have today.

The future of web metrics

> Counting the countable because the countable can be easily counted renders impact illegitimate.
>
> (Brewer, 2011)

This quotation from John Brewer urges us to go beyond what we have traditionally considered sufficient in order to measure and understand our impact on the web. In recognizing that not all relevant data is numbers, we must ask ourselves what it is that we really want to measure. In many ways web and social media metrics provide us with both a challenge and an opportunity. Currently the focus is on the easy access that they provide to numbers, which may discourage us from doing any harder digging (think about how easy it is to log into Google Analytics and stop there); but they also open up a whole new world of metrics where the boundaries are hard to imagine. Indeed, web and social media metrics are already changing many of the more familiar types of metrics used by cultural and scholarly institutions.

Impact metrics probably don't come much more embedded in an institutional culture than does the Journal Impact Factor, which is used by academics and academic institutions to understand the impact of scholarly journals and their articles. Yet, even here there are attempts to reconfigure the picture painted by impact, through initiatives such as alternative metrics or Altmetrics, which aims to take into account both traditional metrics and social media metrics and wider web data. If the web enables broader dissemination of scholarly literature, then it makes sense to understand the wider impact of that content and the ways in which it may be informing policy and the wider society.

Initiatives like Altmetrics are not only beginning to redefine what web metrics might mean within the scholarly environment; they are also beginning to push the boundaries of what is considered relevant data and our thinking about how we can systematize the collection of 'alternative' data and build its use into the strategic missions and activities of our institutions. But, as the following two case studies highlight, just managing 'the numbers' is still a significant task. The case studies demonstrate the need for further strategic thinking about what needs to be collected and why. As Malde et al. make clear in the second case study:

> this challenge is absolutely not about technology … it is first and foremost about audience and the ways in which digital technologies are changing their behaviours: at work, at home, on the move, learning, playing, questioning, socializing, sharing, communicating. Forever.

CASE STUDY 5.1

The web impact of cultural heritage institutions
David Stuart (King's College London)

Introduction
Cultural heritage institutions (CHIs) are increasingly as much interested in the impact of their online content as in that of their physical content. Libraries want to know not only the numbers of books loaned, but also how users are accessing items in institutional repositories; museums and galleries want to know not only the numbers of visitors through the door, but also of those viewing the collections online; and archives are interested not only in which items are being consulted in the reading room but also in how the online finding aids and records are being used. CHIs want to understand how their users are engaging with their online services, and this means understanding

not just how they are engaging with a site, but what they are saying about its content.

The online presence of most CHIs is increasingly complex, both multi-faceted and dynamic. CHIs are using an increasing number of platforms to engage with users. As well as its long-established website and online catalogue a CHI may have a blog or an institutional repository. It may host a variety of formal and informal publications and research outputs, from conference and journal preprints to large datasets and computer code. It may have one or more accounts associated with many of the big social media websites to promote and share its services and resources: it might publish introductory videos to resources on YouTube; share image collections via Flickr; promote events on Facebook; and answer queries on Twitter. If an institution is to understand its impact and improve its service, then it needs not only to collect data from a wide variety of sources, but to understand this data and implement changes on the basis of its findings.

This case study introduces some of the many ways that CHIs may measure their web presence. As will quickly become apparent, many different tools are available that provide access to a seemingly endless array of metrics that can be contrasted and compared. The appropriateness of any particular metric will depend on the reasons for using a specific technology and for measuring the impact – with some being irrelevant or even misleading in certain situations.

The case study starts with a brief overview of some reasons why CHIs may want to measure their web impact. Its main focus is on the online impact of five cultural institutions: the British Museum, the National Gallery, the Natural History Museum, the British Library and the UK National Archives. After introducing the five CHIs and highlighting certain aspects of their online impact that they may be interested to measure, the case study provides an overview of some methods and tools for investigating an organization's online impact. These are grouped into two types: those that provide insights into users' online browsing behaviour and those that can be used to investigate the traces users leave online. The conclusion summarizes the most pertinent issues related to measuring the web impact of an organization, and ends with a list of top tips.

Why measure web impact?

As will quickly become clear, with so many potential web metrics available for analysis, it is essential to have a clear understanding of why the analyst is measuring web impact – if they are to pick an appropriate metric. Behn (2003) has identified eight reasons for managers within a public organization to measure performance, and they are all equally applicable to the investigation of a CHI's web presence. They are: to evaluate, to control, to budget, to motivate, to promote, to celebrate, to learn and to improve.

Evaluation is most organizations' primary motive for measuring their web impact. While an organization's desire to understand how well it is performing will not be limited to evaluating the impact of its web presence, the explicit quantitative metrics that are obtainable using new web technologies may provide more insight than qualitative indicators that rely on the organization's long-established experience or face-to-face interaction with clients.

Controlling is ensuring that employees are doing the right thing. This can include assessing whether an appropriate amount of content is being created, or whether the right balance is being struck between the formal and less formal content that is often combined on social media.

Budgeting, whether of money or time, is an essential function in any organization, and while there are many web services and technologies that are free at the point of use (e.g. Facebook, Twitter, Tumblr), the time spent on one service is necessarily time that is not being spent elsewhere.

Motivation to achieve particular goals can be aided by web metrics. Fuzzy concepts such as 'improve user engagement' can be replaced by specific goals that can be aimed for, such as 'add one hundred new followers'.

Promotion is the use of web metrics to demonstrate the impact of a service to those outside the organization, whether they be the public, journalists or public officials. This is important for CHIs not only in the public sector, where public funding has been under increasing pressure in recent years, but also within the private sector, where information services may need to demonstrate the contribution they are making to the wider organization.

Celebration provides another opportunity to use web metrics in measuring performance. The celebration of notable milestones, whether the 10,000th follower on Twitter or the 1,000th 'Like' on Facebook, provides an opportunity to bring people together and recognize their achievements.

Learning is about understanding why something is or is not working. Evaluation is generally the primary purpose of many web metrics, but it is not enough to know that a technology is or is not a success; it is important to understand *why* it is a success.

Improving services is our eighth reason for using web metrics. It is not enough for CHIs to understand what is or is not working, or why it is or is not working; rather, they need to understand how to change behaviours so that services are improved. However successful an organization's online presence may be, there will always be room for improvement.

In addition to these internally focused motives, web metrics may also be used to help filter the ever-increasing information deluge and to research the behaviour of people who spend an increasing proportion of their lives online

(Stuart, 2014). Although the focus in this chapter is on the CHI measuring its own impact, it is important to recognize that many of the tools and methodologies have wider applications: Twitter can not only give insights into public attitudes to a CHI, but can also play a role in epidemiological research, where it can, for example, give us real-time indicators of flu-like illnesses (Achrekar et al., 2011) and in scientific impact research, where it can be an early indicator of citations (Eysenbach, 2011) and can be used to help filter scientific articles.

Tool categorization

There are a wide range of tools and methodologies for measuring the web impact of an organization's or individual's online content. They may be broadly categorized into four types:

- *User behaviour/user traces*: There are tools that give insights into the way people browse or search the web, and tools that provide insights into the content they leave behind.
- *Internal/external*: There are data-collection tools that an organization incorporates into their content, and external tools that collect data automatically.
- *Private/public*: There are tools where the information is private, and tools where the information is public.
- *Free/subscription*: There are tools that are free at the point of use, and tools that require a subscription. Many of the latter have a freemium model, providing some information for free and some for a price.

The internal/external distinction has much in common with the private/public distinction, although they are not identical. An organization may use internal software to collect information about how users are accessing its web servers, but equally, it may choose to make that information public.

The focus of this case study is primarily on public and free (or at least freemium) tools and methodologies. Some of the tools and metrics considered here are shown in Figure 5.1, categorized according to whether they are internal or external, and whether they make use of user behaviour or user traces.

Considering the web presence of five CHIs

The specific aspects of web impact that are of interest to any one CHI will vary considerably according to its type, the web technologies in use and the ways that they are used. Among the wide variety of institutions and

	User Behaviour	User Traces
Internal	• Page views • Hits	• Comments • Feedback • Contributions
External	• Google searches • Traffic rank • Social media views	• Web mentions • Inlinks/URL citations • Facebook likes • Social network friends

Figure 5.1 *Web metrics tools and methodologies considered by this case study*

technologies, the many different ways that the same technology may be used and the many different tools for measuring variations on the theme of impact, the topic of measuring the web impact of CHIs could easily fill many books.

The five CHIs considered within this chapter are the British Museum, the National Gallery, the Natural History Museum, the British Library and the UK National Archives. Like many large organizations that have had a web presence for a (relatively) long time, each of these CHIs has a large and multi-faceted web presence. As well as core information about its work and events, a CHI's web pages will often include a wide range of educational and learning materials, online catalogues, virtual collections, online stores, links to a wide range of external social media services and, increasingly, institutional datasets.

The review of our five CHIs' web presences does not aim to be comprehensive, but is designed to demonstrate the variety of technologies and services both provided and used, and to aid a discussion of how they may be measured.

User behaviour: internal

User behaviour is the aspect of impact that most people will think of when considering measures of web impact, as seen in the use of log analysis or page tagging. Log analysis uses the server logs from the hosting server to analyse the files that have been requested by browsers or, increasingly, automatic agents. Page tagging involves the inclusion of some JavaScript code within each web page to provide an analytics program with information about pages that have been requested. This is most often done with Google Analytics.

Both log analysis and page tagging have their limitations. Log analysis is possible only where the organization has direct access to the server logs, whereas page tagging may be incorporated into blogs, wikis and content management systems hosted on external servers. For page tagging to provide information about which pages have been requested, JavaScript must be enabled in the user's browser; and it will provide no information about a resource that is accessed as an embedded item hosted on the server of another organization. Most importantly, neither page tagging nor log analysis provides suitable bench-marking information, as the data they generate is generally accessible only to the organization that owns the website and other organization's data will not be available for comparison. However, self-referential comparisons can be made over time; for example, Figure 5.2 shows the rise (and fall) in the number of hits received by the UK Government Web Archive.

Analytics software generally captures data about the visitor, the content they view and the source they come from. This enables a seemingly endless range of metrics from the general (e.g. number of visits to a site) to the specific (e.g. number of visits to a particular page, by an iPhone 4 user in Turkey, on a particular day using particular keywords). Often it's the global metrics that gain the most attention: 'X million page views' or 'Top 10 search terms'. However, while these may be useful for promotional or celebratory purposes, more specific metrics can play an important role in the evaluation or improvement of particular aspects of a website, such as:

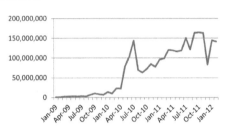

Figure 5.2
'Hits' received by the UK Government Web Archive hosted by the National Archives (National Archives, 2012)

- Does a large number of page views represent interest in the content, or users' inability to find the information they need?
- Are people reading all the pages in a particular series, or dropping out half way through?

Generally, most of this information is kept in-house, and if analytics information is shared more widely it is only the top-line numbers. Even there, however, it is important to remember that different software will calculate the numbers in different ways, and comparisons between publicly declared figures may not be comparing like with like.

User behaviour: external
Comparisons of users' behaviour with content from different CHIs can be made by using global traffic statistics as well as behavioural metrics on social media websites.

Global traffic services

A number of services provide insights into web traffic across the web: Alexa (www.alexa.com), Compete (www.compete.com), Quantcast (www.quantcast. com). These generally operate with a freemium model: some information is available for free, while the full service often requires a subscription. Each of the services not only provides access to different information, but collects the information in different ways: Alexa's ranking information is based on users of the Alexa toolbar, as well as a sample of all internet users (Alexa, 2014); Compete's information is based on a sample of 2 million US internet users (Compete, 2014); Quantcast provides a web analytics and advertising service, collecting data from 'Quantified' sites and estimating traffic for other sites (Quantcast, 2014).

Unlike an internal service such as Google Analytics, external services enable comparisons between multiple institutions, although they do not generally enable the same level of detail that a website owner can get for their own site and it can be difficult to determine the traffic for sites that don't have their own domain name. Table 5.1 shows the visitor numbers and Alexa Traffic Rank for the five CHIs discussed in this chapter.

Table 5.1 *Visitor numbers and Alexa Traffic Rank for five CHIs*			
Cultural Heritage Institution	**Visitors in 2013 (ALVA, 2014)**	**Alexa Traffic Rank – global**	**Alexa Traffic Rank – UK**
British Museum (www.britishmuseum.org)	6,701,036	45,638	3,878
National Gallery (www.nationalgallery.org.uk)	6,031,574	99,861	9,971
Natural History Museum (www.nhm.ac.uk)	5,356,884	55,835	4,797
British Library (www.bl.uk)	1,475,382	26,008	2,246
National Archives (www.nationalarchives.gov.uk)	93,000*	17,031	809
Note: * www.lboro.ac.uk/microsites/infosci/lisu/lampost09/visits09.html#archvis			

Comparisons with other websites give meaning to relatively meaningless numbers such as 150,000,000 'hits'. The National Archives is the highest-ranking of the five CHIs considered in this chapter, despite having the lowest number of real-world visitors. It is important to recognize, however, that even the National Archives website ranks fairly low in comparison to many other websites.

There are many possible reasons for the relatively low ranking of CHIs' websites: online engagement is not considered a priority for the CHIs; limitations in the data collection methodology adversely affect CHI rankings; or simply that other websites are just more interesting. It is not necessarily important for a CHI to have a top-ranking website, or even to be ranked well in comparison to other, similar institutions, but understanding how a site ranks in comparison to those of similar organizations can lead to a discussion on whether or not a website is achieving its objectives.

Google Trends

Another source of information about the impact of institutions on the web is Google Trends. Rather than providing information about the pages people are visiting, it can provide insights into what people are searching for. This allows for insights into the impact of particular exhibitions or events.

Figure 5.3 shows that despite an overall decline in the number of searches for the British Museum since 2004, there is a clear spike in September 2007. This coincides with an exhibition about China's Terracotta Army, and indeed correlates with a rise in the number of searches for 'terracotta army'. It is important to remember that while the decline in the number of searches for the British Museum could reflect a decrease in interest in the British Museum, there are other possible reasons. For example, the site's domain name may have become so well known that people go to it directly rather than searching for it; alternatively (and probably more likely in this case), it may reflect the way the data is calculated. Rather than providing information about the absolute number of web searches, Google normalizes the data by the volume of searches (Google, 2014). This means that as internet use and Google Search have reached an increasingly diverse range of people, with different interests and using different languages, we can expect English terms to account for an increasingly smaller proportion of searches; indeed, the decay rate for a number of English words has been noted (e.g. Hubbard, 2011). Figure 5. 3 is based on global interest in the British Museum; a similar graph restricted to the UK alone shows a far smaller decline.

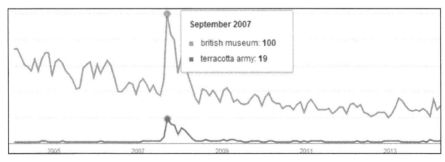

Figure 5.3 *'British Museum' and 'Terracotta Army' as seen through Google Trends*

Social media views

Increasingly, many organizations have a presence on a wide range of external social media websites. Table 5.2 shows the social media services that are prominently promoted by each of the five CHIs. There are likely to be additional accounts for particular workers, teams or projects, accounts on other platforms and accounts that are no longer used. It is important to recognize that even where a CHI doesn't create a social media account itself, it may nonetheless have web pages created automatically or by other web users on social media and sharing sites and services. For example, while the British Library is the only one of our five CHIs that links to TripAdvisor (a reviews website for attractions and tourist destinations), TripAdvisor pages exist for each of the institutions. In each case, the pages would have been created by a user who had visited the institution and wanted to let others know what the experience had been like.

Table 5.2 *Prominent social media of the five CHIs*	
Cultural heritage institution	**Social media site**
The British Museum (www.britishmuseum.org)	Facebook, Twitter, YouTube, Flickr
National Gallery (www.nationalgallery.org.uk)	Facebook, Twitter, YouTube, Google Plus
Natural History Museum (www.nhm.ac.uk)	Facebook, Twitter, YouTube
British Library (www.bl.uk)	Facebook, Twitter, YouTube, Google Plus, Pinterest, TripAdvisor
National Archives (www.nationalarchives.gov.uk)	Facebook, Twitter, YouTube, Flickr, Wikimedia Commons

The social media services often promote a wide range of metrics, predominantly displaying information about a user's number of followers, views and the amount of content that has been created.

Where an organization is sharing content, it is likely to be interested in the number of views that content has received. Facebook, YouTube and Flickr each provide view-based metrics, while social media providers rely on associated metrics such as number of followers or number of shares. Facebook provides information on the number of visitors to a page and the most visitors in a week; YouTube provides information about views per video as well as views for a whole account; Flickr provides information about how often each photo is viewed, requiring the user to aggregate this information.

As with comparisons of all web content, it is important to compare like with like and to recognize the different uses to which a technology is put. For example, Flickr is used by the British Museum primarily for promotional purposes, while the National Archives and the British Library both participate in the Flickr Commons, a project to share public image archives. Whereas the

British Library has uploaded over 1 million images and the National Archives around 20,000, many of which have been viewed thousands of times, the British Museum has shared fewer than 2,000 images, many of which have been viewed only a handful of times. This does not mean that the British Museum account is not a success; indeed questions would probably be raised about where resources were being applied if thousands of people had been encouraged to view images of the members' Christmas party! Equally, another institution's account designed to share cultural images more widely cannot be considered successful just because its images have been viewed more often than those of the British Museum. This merely emphasizes the importance of identifying the metrics that matter for a particular CHI, and comparing like with like.

User traces: internal

Hits and page views have traditionally been the focus of web analytic investigations; however, the increasing adoption of social media sites and services provides the potential for investigating stronger levels of engagement. For example, a page view is quite a low indicator of engagement between a user and a site's web content, in comparison to the traces that users leave behind on the web. Comments and links not only show a stronger level of user engagement but also provide a rich source of information about the nature of the engagement.

In this chapter 'user traces' refers to impressions left on the web deliberately, and generally these can be captured retrospectively by anyone with the necessary technology. User *behaviour* must be captured at the time, either by the user (e.g. via the Alexa toolbar) or by the website (e.g. by Google Analytics), and access is controlled by the owner of the data. Whereas some data owners share some of this information widely in a suitably anonymized format (e.g. Alexa and Google), much of it is not shared. In comparison, user *traces* remain available for investigation until the trace is either changed or deleted. As with user behaviour, investigations of user traces may be either internal or external; a CHI can focus either on the comments or contributions made to its own website, or on those left on the wider web. It would be a challenge to do both sufficiently well.

Blogs

Blogs are one of the most established social media technologies, providing a simple mechanism for regularly updating a website with posts that are published in reverse chronological order, and are widely used in the cultural heritage sector. They may be associated with specific projects, specific areas of work or an institution as a whole. Of the five CHIs considered in this chapter, four have at least one prominently displayed blog. Both the British Museum (http://blog.britishmuseum.org) and the National Archives (http://blog.nationalarchives.gov.uk) have general blogs, while the blog pages of the British Library (www.bl.uk/blogs) and the Natural History Museum (www.nhm.ac.uk/natureplus) bring together a wide range of blogs by people within the institution and, in the case of the Natural History Museum, also forums. Importantly, blogs aren't only a means for publishing information, but are a means of obtaining feedback.

Comments are the feature that distinguishes blogs from other content management systems. They enable organizations not only to show the work that they are doing, but also to engage in conversation with users. However, even for something as seemingly simple as comments, multiple metrics may be calculated, and while each may be appropriate for a particular situation they also have their own limitations:

- *Number of comments*: these will vary a great deal, according to the number of posts posted.
- *Number of comments per post*: the raw number of comments can easily be increased by removing any moderation.
- *Number of positive comments*: Content analysis or automatic sentiment analysis is necessary to determine the reasons for the number of comments, and even then the result could be adversely affected by a number of users posting multiple times.
- *Number of commentators per post*: this may be inflated by the posting of contentious issues.

Crowdsourcing applications

Blogs are not the only way users can contribute to CHI websites, as CHIs look for ways to gain contributions from the wider community on specific projects. For example, as well as a Creative Commons project on Flickr, the British Library has also hosted its own crowdsourcing Georeference project designed to make digitized maps from the collection available in the most accessible format (www.bl.uk/maps), while the Natural History Museum is a partner in the Notes from Nature (www.notesfromnature.org) Zooniverse project to engage the public in transcribing historical records from the museum.

Unlike many activities, these projects have definitive goals. Although there are many additional metrics that may be calculated (e.g. number of contributors, average number of contributions per contributor) the completion of the project is the primary goal. However, if the project is part of a wider move towards crowdsourcing, then there may be greater interest in both the numbers and the demographics of contributors, and to improve both of these it is necessary to consider opinion on the web more widely.

User traces: external

The power of the web comes from the fact that content and websites do not exist in isolation but, rather, are interconnected. The web can be viewed as a giant conversation with people talking about and linking to the content of other organizations. Originally these conversations happened across the web on millions of small websites, but increasingly they happen within a small number of huge social media websites with hundreds of millions of users. Both the web as a whole and large social media sites need to be considered when investigating the impact of a CHI.

The traditional web

The web in general is not as consistently structured as are the profiles on social media sites, and similar information is likely to be found not only in different places on different websites, but also on different pages within the same website. This lack of consistency means that measures of impact have focused on two types of information that can be readily discerned: the text of web pages and the links between web pages.

Web impact assessment

A web impact assessment refers to assessing the impact of ideas or documents by counting the number of times they are mentioned online (Thelwall, 2009). For the CHI interested in its online impact, a web impact assessment may be considered a methodological approach to searching on itself.

At the most basic level, the assessment may be of the number of hits a particular search gets when entered into a search engine. Table 5.3 shows the estimated number of results displayed on Google.com when doing a phrase search for each of the five CHIs.

Table 5.3 *Estimated number of results for organizational names in Google*

Phrase search	Results
'British Museum'	3,560,000
'National Gallery'	4,070,000
'Natural History Museum'	23,000,000
'British Library'	7,770,000
'National Archives'	9,580,000

Although web impact assessments undoubtedly have the potential to provide some insights into ideas or documents, limitations of the current web as well as the current generation of search tools means that the applicability of web impact assessments is quite limited.

The disadvantage of the current web is that most of its content is not semantically enriched; HTML (HyperText Markup Language) is generally used to tell web browsers how data should be displayed, not to distinguish between any ambiguities that may be inherent due to the use of homonyms. Phrase searching for the five CHIs is likely to return numerous pages that, while including the particular text, aren't referring to the national CHIs in the United Kingdom. A search for 'National Archives', for instance, also returns pages from many other national archives around the world.

Even when the phrase search is less likely to be ambiguous, for example, for distinct publication titles, it is nevertheless important to remember that the search result is only one version of the web operationalized through one particular tool. Search engines do not index the whole of the web. Not only do they prioritize indexing some parts over others, but some of the technologies used to build websites, the structure of the web itself and its dynamic nature preclude any site from indexing the whole of the web. The number of results provided by search engines are generally not exact but, rather, estimations, and the estimated number of results on the first page of the results can be significantly different from the estimated number of results on the tenth page. Among the CHIs in this study, 'Natural History Museum' has the highest estimated number of hits, with an estimated 23,000,000, although clicking through the pages of results finds the estimated number quickly falling to 697, even when including pages that Google initially considers too similar.

This does not mean that a web impact assessment can't be useful; it merely highlights the need for a methodological approach. It is important to go through as many pages of results as possible to ensure the most accurate estimate of pages possible, and to classify a sample of those pages that can be seen so as to determine the proportion that actually relate to the specific topic or document.

Inlinks/URL citations

A level of ambiguity is inevitable with text searches, whereas the unique nature of URIs (Uniform Resource Identifiers) should leave no room for ambiguity as multiple organizations are not allowed to have the same domain name. However, the tools available for investigating the links pointing to websites (i.e. inlinks) or specific web pages are quite limited. Whereas link data was once available via the major search engines, this functionality has been depreciated by most search engines. Now such investigations must make use of the functionality provided by tools aimed primarily at search engine optimization specialists, such as ahrefs (http://ahrefs.com), Majestic SEO (www.majesticseo.com) and Open Site Explorer (www.opensiteexplorer. org). Such sites vary in terms of the amount of information that is available for free, with the finer details often restricted.

Table 5.4 compares the number of external inlinks as well as the number of linking domains as identified through ahrefs, Majestic SEO and Open Site Explorer. The number of inlinking domains may be considered more important than the number of inlinking pages, as one site linking to another site multiple times (e.g. linking to every record in a database, or having a link on every page of a blog) could adversely skew the results. The different sites show a large variation in both the number of inlinks and the number of domains identified. This means that the CHI making the biggest impact in terms of links could variously be identified as the National Archives (ahrefs – links), the British Library (ahrefs – domains; Majestic SEO – inlinks; Majestic SEO – domains) or the British Museum (Open Site Explorer – inlinks; Open Site Explorer – domains)!

Although ahrefs, Majestic SEO and Open Site Explorer each provide access to the raw figures for free, automated access and access to details of the specific pages or domains that are linking in is often available only at a premium. Nevertheless, this information is important if a person wants to

Table 5.4 *The number of inlinks and linking domains for the five CHIs according to three different SEO sites*

CHI	ahrefs		Majestic SEO		Open Site Explorer	
	External inlinks	Referring domains	External inlinks	Referring domains	External inlinks	Referring domains
The British Museum (www. britishmuseum.org)	4,520,262	25,720	1,736,392	25,170	92,056	8,353
National Gallery (www.nationalgallery .org.uk)	554,491	18,803	654,692	18,556	42,568	5,599
Natural History Museum (www.nhm.ac.uk)	1,083,140	27,900	3,191,886	29,073	59,086	5,997
British Library (www.bl.uk)	2,658,862	34,313	12,532,308	33,873	72,025	7,662
National Archives (www. nationalarchives.gov. uk)	5,774,571	20,817	3,601,244	21,384	52,696	3,845

perform a content analysis on the reasons why links are being placed or to consider the wider network of relationships. This may still be achieved for free by the use of a variation of the web link, the URL citation.

A URL citation is the appearance of a URI within the text of a page. This means that search engines will index them and can be used to investigate them. For example, "bbc.co.uk" -site:bbc.co.uk is a phrase search to find the appearance of bbc.co.uk in the text of web pages that are not part of the main BBC website, while "bbc.co.uk" site:twitter.com finds the appearance of bbc.co.uk on pages within the Twitter domain. The Webometric Analyst (http://lexiurl.wlv.ac.uk) software from the Statistical Cybermetrics Research Group at the University of Wolverhampton is designed for the collection and analysis of data from a wide range of online sources, including the search engine Bing, the last of the major search engines to allow automatic querying of its search engine. Automating the combining of URI citations on multiple web domains enables the production of network diagrams between the different websites.

Figure 5.4 shows a directed network diagram of URL citations between the five CHIs, with the size of the arrows reflecting the number of URI citations from one site to another. This is based on data collected via Webometric Analyst and displayed through the Gephi (https://gephi.org) visualization software. The British Library and the UK National Archives can be seen to be the most strongly interconnected. Where a particular network of actors are considered particularly significant, analysis may make use of social network analysis concepts such as betweenness centrality, closeness centrality and eigenvector centrality to provide alternative insights into the most central node within a network.

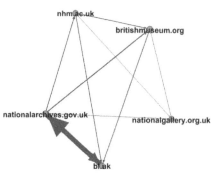

Figure 5.4
Network diagram of URL citations between five CHIs

We return to this below, with reference to social media metrics.

Social media metrics

People aren't just consuming content on the web, they are creating content, sharing content and having conversations, in both their personal and professional lives. These traces provide a rich source of information for investigation and, in comparison to the diversity of traditional web pages, social network sites create a large amount of data that is structured in the same format. This has led to the creation of a number of desktop tools and web services available for both collecting and analysing this data.

Impact of web content on social media sites

As well as investigating the impact of content on the web as a whole, it is also possible to investigate the impact of content on a small part of it. Both ahrefs and Open Site Explorer currently provide access to social metrics about the impact of web metrics, although of the two only ahrefs provides access to this data for free, and even then only sharing the number of Google +1s, Tweets, Facebook Likes, and Facebook shares for a website's homepage (Table 5.5).

Table 5.5 *Impact of websites on social media platforms*

CHI	Google +1s	Twitter Tweets	Facebook Likes	Facebook Shares
The British Museum (www.britishmuseum.org)	662	1,500	2,200	3,500
National Gallery (www.nationalgallery.org.uk)	2,200	687	1,600	2,300
Natural History Museum (www.nhm.ac.uk)	5,000	684	1,100	2,200
British Library (www.bl.uk)	27,000	1,500	1,100	2,000
National Archives (www.nationalarchives.gov.uk)	26	315	570	1,300

However, there are also further means of investigating impact on a specific service. In some cases there is a simple, user-friendly web service adding additional search functionality to a site's service. For example, Topsy (http://topsy.com) provides a more extensive search service for Twitter content than is provided by Twitter itself. Many social media sites also have extensive APIs (application programming interfaces), allowing developers and researchers to automatically download vast quantities of data. However, most people interested in investigating social media content are unlikely to have the necessary programming skills to capture this data for themselves, but there are tools that provide a more accessible user interface to the APIs. These are discussed below in the context of measuring the impact of social media content itself.

Impact of social media content

No other web content is seemingly as aligned with web metrics as that on social media sites. Users are not only encouraged to follow, share and comment on one another's content, but the associated metrics are often prominently displayed, whether this be the number of followers on Twitter or the number of times a video has been liked on YouTube. It is important to remember, however, that not only is the nearest metric not necessarily the best, but also consideration should be given not only to the content that is captured but also the content that isn't.

For instance, one of the most noticeable pieces of social content is the Facebook 'Like', enabling users to simply respond positively to content that has been put online. There is, however, no equivalent 'dislike' or 'ambivalent' button on Facebook. Users may comment negatively about the content that is shared, but this is not reflected in the simplicity of metrics that revolve around the number of 'Likes' a post has received. Equally, following someone on Twitter gives little indication of why they are followed, and retweets are not endorsements. Tools that enable the downloading of content via social media sites can provide more nuanced insights into the impact of a CHI's account and the nature of the impact.

One way that a more nuanced understanding of impact can be achieved is through the methods of social network analysis. These can enable the identification of clusters, describe the structure of the network as a whole or provide metrics for the impact of the particular nodes in the network. Social networking sites often highlight one such indicator of the impact of a node in the network in the form of the number of followers or friends. This is the equivalent of the social network analysis concept of 'degree centrality', the number of other nodes that a node has linking to it. There are also other measures of centrality that consider the network more widely:

- *Closeness centrality* gives high centrality to those that can quickly interact with other nodes.
- *Betweenness centrality* gives high centrality to those nodes that lie on the shortest paths between other pairs of nodes.
- *Eigenvector centrality*, like the associated *PageRank*, gives high centrality to those nodes that are connected to highly connected nodes.

Figure 5.5 provides a network diagram of the five CHIs, along with those other CHIs in the 20 most-visited attractions in the UK in 2013. The data has been collected through the Twitter API, then analysed with the open source graph visualization software Gephi (https://gephi.org). The Excel spreadsheet template NodeXL (http://nodexl.codeplex.com) and Webometrics Analyst (http://lexiurl.wlv.ac.uk) provide simple interfaces for downloading data from a number of social networking sites, although it is important to have a clear understanding of exactly what is being downloaded, as the functionality of the tools often changes as the sites' functionality changes.

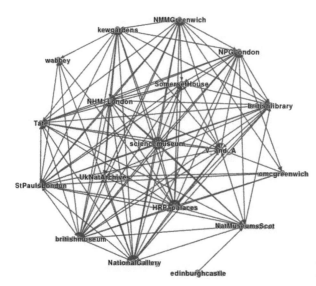

Figure 5.5
*Social network of the UK's
most-visited CHIs*

Table 5.6 shows the different measures of centrality for each of the five CHIs within this network. Although the British Library has the most followers on Twitter, of the five CHIs it is the British Museum that has in-degree, betweenness centrality and eigenvector centrality from the small select network.

When the costs of creating content on the web are relatively low, it is important to consider the value of connections as part of a wider context. The number of connections is as likely to reflect the quantity of content and time on a site, as it is to reflect quality of content, so it is important to consider the value of the connections. Where the metrics revolve around the number of comments or mentions a site receives, the value of the content can be assessed through a content analysis or sentiment analysis of a sample of the content.

Table 5.6 *Total Twitter followers and centrality of the five CHIs*					
CHI	Total Twitter followers	In-degree	Closeness centrality	Betweenness centrality	Eigenvector centrality
British Museum (@britishmuseum)	300,415	15	1.00	24.50	1.00
National Gallery (@nationalgallery)	221,796	12	1.06	8.13	0.88
Natural History Museum (@nhm_london)	531,811	13	1.23	8.68	0.92
British Library (@britishlibrary)	559,552	12	1.25	4.62	0.81
National Archives (@uknatarchives)	36,751	8	1.81	0.50	0.55

A semantic web

As well as a seemingly endless variety of metrics for the websites and social media sites that contribute to many CHIs' web presence, the ways that we use the web continue to change. Today CHIs are increasingly interested in sharing data online. In some cases this is as Excel spreadsheets, or even PDFs, but the real power of the web comes from releasing the data in the standards of the semantic web and linking to other public datasets. This requires new tools and new metrics for understanding the impact of both the data that is published and the way that it is published.

Both the British Library and the British Museum have published significant datasets as Linked Open Data (i.e. publicly shared and linked datasets according to the standards of the Semantic Web). The British Library has published its British National Biography (http://bnb.data.bl.uk) and the British Museum has made its catalogue available online (http://collection.britishmuseum.org), both according to Semantic Web standards. As well as the number of times semantic content has been requested from a server, the impact of the content may also be considered in terms of how other datasets link to their content using tools such as the Semantic Web index Sindice (http://sindice.com).

It is important to consider not only the impact of the data, but also the data models and element sets to which the data conforms. For example, as well as publishing the British National Bibliography, the British Library has also published its data model, the particular selection of elements that the British Library has chosen for structuring the bibliographic information. Some of the elements have been appropriated from other organizations' schemas and some have been defined by the British Library itself. Understanding the impact of the British Library's online content means understanding the reuse of its elements and data model as well.

Conclusion

CHIs' presences, and understanding the impact of their content on different platforms, requires multiple approaches and tools. This case study has mentioned a few of these tools and metrics, but it has hardly scratched the surface. Whereas once the problem might have been finding things to count, today the problem is selecting the most appropriate things to count.

There will inevitably be a tendency to reach for those metrics that are most accessible, and while it may be the case that the most accessible metric is the most suitable metric, it is nonetheless important to recognize that every metric has limitations. In most situations a handful of metrics should be selected to provide an insight into impact and, to misquote Kipling, let all the selected metrics count with you, but none too much. No single metric will necessarily provide a true picture of a CHI's web impact but, rather, they should be used as the beginning of a conversation, and those putting together such a narrative should be aware of the alternatives.

Top tips

1   **Track things that matter**
    Many different metrics are available, but that doesn't mean you want to know them all. Unless a researcher is selective, they will quickly find themselves drowning in numbers.
2   **The most accessible metric is not necessarily the best**
    Some metrics are simple to calculate, and others may be heavily promoted, but it's important that the investigators consider the appropriateness of a metric to their situation.
3   **Every tool has limitations**
    Some tools will give limited information, and some will give inaccurate information. It is important to understand the limitations of the tool, what it can tell you and what it can't.
4   **Accept the fact that tools will change**
    As tools and sites change, so will the metrics that can be investigated. Measuring the impact of web content requires regularly looking for new and innovative solutions for identifying useful new metrics.
5   **No metric ever tells the whole story**

CASE STUDY 5.2

Let's Get Real: a Journey Towards Understanding and Measuring Digital Engagement

Sejul Malde (Culture24), Jane Finnis (Culture24), Anra Kennedy (Culture24), Elena Villaespesa (Tate), Seb Chan (Cooper-Hewitt Smithsonian National Design Museum, NY) and Mia Ridge (Open University)

Introduction

The times they are a-changin'. Digital tools have worked their way into every aspect of our lives. Those people with high levels of digital fluency take for granted the increased levels of speed, access and mobility that as little as three years ago were hard to imagine. For many, the possibilities still feel a little bit sci-fi-esque, but, as William Gibson observed so insightfully in 2003, 'the future is already here – it's just not evenly distributed'. This is as true in the cultural sector as it is for anyone, with many organizations struggling to embrace the new reality of audience behaviour, let alone go boldly into a future of big data, the Semantic Web and seamless participation.

But this challenge is absolutely not about technology, which we are often guilty of fetishizing as a solution to problems. It is first and foremost about audience and the ways in which digital technologies are changing their behaviours: at work, at home, on the move, learning, playing, questioning, socializing, sharing, communicating. Forever.

This case study grapples with this shift in behaviours and tries to make sense of it on behalf of arts and heritage organizations. It summarizes Culture24's Let's Get Real Phase 2 project: A Journey Towards Understanding and Measuring Digital Engagement. It tells the story that emerges from taking the time to think, to question, to measure and to analyse.

Background

In 2010, when Culture24 was setting up the first Let's Get Real project (Phase 1: How to Evaluate Online Success) one of the key questions we tackled was how to meaningfully integrate digital tactics into a cultural organization's overall strategic mission. This sounds obvious but it is not as simple as it may at first appear.

The starting point for our second phase of action research work was the 2011 Let's Get Real report and findings. This report was the outcome of Culture24's first collaborative action research project, How to Evaluate Online Success, which took place between June 2010 and September 2011 and involved 17 UK cultural venues. The frankness of this report and its openness in speaking about the failure in the cultural sector to really capture the attention of online audiences was met by a very positive reaction. It has sparked interest within the cultural sector in the UK and internationally, and presentations about the findings have been given at DISH 2012, Museums & Web 2012, Bits2Blogs 2012, British Council Sino-UK Creative Economy Forum and others. The report itself has also been quoted and shared widely, and it was downloaded over 11,000 times between October 2010 and June 2013.

For many cultural organizations, the online world and digital tools are still unfamiliar and unknown. They are aware of the knowledge gap between them and those (often younger) individuals who feel fluent in the new language. This tension is made worse by the fact that although digital technologies are understood as tools that need to be used and shaped to a purpose, they also change the very nature of their users' behaviour – allowing access to information on the move, facilitating connections between sets of previously separate data and offering a multitude of opportunities for sharing and participation.

As such, the change needed in order for an organization to feel confident in understanding these changes in user behaviour and then to integrate the use of digital tactics into its overall strategic mission in useful ways requires a significant shift in internal thinking at all levels. The time, space and commitment needed to do this well cannot be under-estimated.

Many cultural organizations also face a raft of internal pressures sparked by expectations such as:

• Online developments will significantly improve audience reach
• Online developments will provide access to new audiences (especially younger ones)
• We need to be seen to be using digital tools and not getting left behind
• Senior management (directors/trustees) wants us to build a big, shiny new showcase digital 'thing' that will show everyone we are cool (app, kiosk, game, etc.)
• Digital will help us earn more money
• Digital will increase participation.

These expectations are often unrealistic and are strategically the wrong starting place for thinking about any new business development of any kind, but especially any using digital technologies. The starting point should, instead, be the mission of the organization and the needs of the target audience. You need to know what you want to achieve and whom it is for. A useful entry point for each cultural organization to explore how its organizational missions can connect with the needs of its target audiences online is to examine the question 'what is digital engagement?'

Once an organization begins to understand this question, the key internal challenge then becomes one of digital literacy and technical capability among the staff team as they try to choose the right platform, channel or approach to do what they want to do. The journey becomes essentially one of internal change that is geared to nurturing digitally fluent staff and, crucially, digitally fluent decision makers.

This action research project, led by Culture24 and involving 22 participating cultural organizations collaborating over an 11-month period, explored what digital engagement could mean for them. Each organization in the project was supported through the process of considering this question in more detail in order to try to focus it on segmenting its audience and setting more specific objectives.

The project provided a very welcome opportunity to step back from the day-to-day issues of delivering digital services and to instead reflect upon the wider issues, while learning and sharing with colleagues and experts.

This case study summarizes the journey for the 22 project partners, facilitated by the Culture24 project team. We hope that the recommendations and learning provide invaluable insights and a snapshot of the wider struggle that the cultural sector faces to significantly improve its digital services.

Project background

The Let's Get Real Phase 2 project brought together 22 partner cultural organizations for four face-to-face workshops, supplemented by online discussion, review and analysis, over a period of 11 months between July 2012 and May 2013. The partner organizations were:

- Amgueddfa Cymru – National Museum Wales
- Birmingham Museums
- Brighton Museum and Art Gallery
- Bristol Museums, Galleries and Archives
- British Library
- British Museum
- Historic Royal Palaces
- National Museums Scotland
- The Photographers' Gallery
- Polka Theatre
- Museum of London
- National Galleries of Scotland
- Own Art
- REcreative
- Science Museum
- Shakespeare's Globe
- Tate
- Victoria & Albert Museum
- Wales Millennium Centre
- Warwick Arts Centre
- Watershed
- Wellcome Collection.

With cultural organizations' funding becoming tighter, it was more important than ever that investments were made wisely. People needed to make sure that they were investing their time, energy and cash based on an honest evaluation of what worked well, and were committed fully to learning from mistakes. Meaningful insights into the value of online activities were found not in data collected, or in the tools and platforms used for evaluation, but in the shift in thinking that needed to happen at a deep level within every cultural organization. We believed that these lessons could be found only through careful analysis of the data against each organization's primary objectives.

This project took a highly collaborative approach to these issues, and this was mirrored in a collaborative funding model, with each participant contributing £2,500.

The core project team consisted of:

- Jane Finnis, Chief Executive, Culture24
- Sejul Malde, Research Manager, Culture24
- Mia Ridge, Doctoral Researcher, freelance cultural heritage technologist
- Seb Chan, Director of Digital and Emerging Media, Cooper-Hewitt Smithsonian National Design Museum
- Elena Villaespesa, PhD student, University of Leicester.

Culture24's role was to lead and co-ordinate the project and bring in experts as necessary to support all stages of the project delivery.

Mia Ridge and Seb Chan both brought invaluable technical knowledge to the project. They both have significant experience of working with digital issues relating to the cultural sector, and were able to provide expert guidance to participating organizations throughout the project relating to the practical use of technologies to gather data and how to draw meaningful insights from this.

The investigation into social media behaviours which fed into the overall research project was carried out by Elena Villaespesa, Digital Analyst at Tate, and formed part of her PhD work for the School of Museum Studies at the University of Leicester.

Together, the core project team curated the project, carrying out the research, data collection and analysis which was then fed back and acted on by the participating organizations. This formed the basis of the three main areas of research (web, mobile, social) which are summarized later in this case study.

Understanding digital engagement?

The project embarked on its collaborative journey by seeking to interrogate and understand exactly what we thought was meant by 'digital engagement'.

We knew at the outset of the project that seeking to explore a question such as 'what is digital engagement?' for cultural organizations was setting ourselves up for failure. 'Engagement' is one of the most slippery of concepts, meaning many things to many people.

To better understand digital engagement, cultural organizations need to understand what and whom they value, along with what their audiences value, before exploring how these might be enhanced through digital channels.

As a group, we were interested in undertaking a collaborative journey to shed light on these questions. Our aim was not to arrive at a set of unified answers, but instead to derive a way of thinking about the questions in a joined-up and informed manner.

To start this journey we needed to decide as a group which specific lines of enquiry would be useful. We needed to become better informed about existing knowledge about digital engagement from both a macro and micro perspective. For the macro viewpoint, we were keen to find out how other sectors might be approaching the issue. From a micro perspective, we wanted to draw upon the group's existing knowledge, experiences, data and views on digital engagement.

Exploring the macro perspective

Matt Locke, Director of Storythings and former Head of Multiplatform Commissioning at Channel 4, attended the first project group workshop. He spoke about the evolving nature of digital engagement and how commercial organizations such as Channel 4 have transformed their output in order to connect with audiences more meaningfully. Matt reflected on how, in the digital age, organizations have to adapt to the changing attention patterns and behaviours of audiences in order to connect with them more meaningfully.

He presented a potted 'History of the Internet in 41 behaviours' (Locke, 2013), to demonstrate how digital engagement has rapidly changed and expanded audience behaviours. He described how organizations should no longer seek to understand their audiences as rigid personas who behave in a unified way based on static demographics but, rather, as responsive individuals continually adapting their behaviours according to new forms and channels of digital participation.

Matt proposed that one way to define engagement for an organization is through understanding the changing behaviours of its audiences. He went on to explain how organizations that are better at driving engagement look to align their organizational audience goals with key target-audience behaviours. This involves examining which behaviours are needed from audiences in order to achieve these goals, before examining what data organizations have about their ability to perform these behaviours.

Exploring the micro perspective

Following Matt's presentation, the group discussed what engagement meant for each of them by examining and articulating their organizational missions, their potential target behaviours and their digital engagement goals for specific audiences.

Shared issues drawn from these discussions included:

- difficulty in linking the broader organizational mission with specific digital approaches and objectives
- lack of understanding of how to interrogate analytic metrics meaningfully in order to examine digital engagement
- difficulty in defining specific audience-engagement goals in measurable terms
- desire to understand more about their audiences' existing behaviours on digital platforms (before any reflection on target behaviours could be carried out)
- desire to understand the impact of mobile devices on audience behaviours.

We then reflected upon the insights drawn from the micro and macro perspectives described above. This process and the knowledge gained informed the approach we took to interrogating digital engagement more deeply.

From the discussion, the following points were agreed to be important:

- Digital engagement is not separate from other forms of audience engagement.
- The key digital-engagement goals for an organization must be connected to the broader audience-engagement mission of the organization.
- Digital-engagement goals can be interpreted as those that meet the key target-behaviours of audiences, which can take place via digital platforms.
- In order to understand how to meet target behaviours via digital platforms, an organization must have an understanding of its existing audience behaviours taking place on these platforms.
- To track the progress of digital-engagement goals, these should be measurable in some way, and a host of tools and metrics are available that can do this. Their usefulness needs to be interrogated for each organization, based on its broader audience-engagement mission, making it vital to measure what it values as an organization, and not simply to value what it measures.
- The increasing use of mobile technologies and smartphones continues to dramatically change audience behaviour, but the pace of change within cultural organizations is not keeping up with this.

Taking these points together, it was agreed to interrogate engagement further by taking a practical look at the existing behaviours of audiences via three digital channels: web, mobile and social media. This would allow the group to interrogate the usefulness of a variety of metrics for engagement, as well as to examine how those metrics could be linked to broader organizational mission.

Understanding web behaviours

The challenge of understanding and interpreting web analytic metrics more meaningfully, in terms of indicative audience behaviours, was explored by the project group.

Rob Stein, Deputy Director of Dallas Museum of Art, explained the value of combining qualitative audience motivation data with quantitative web metric data in order to obtain a more complete picture of audience behaviour, a value he's been exploring in his own research (Stein et al., 2012). This research identified five key categories of motivation for specific online audiences:

1   Plan a visit to the museum.
2   Find specific information for research or professional purposes.
3   Find specific information for personal interest.
4   Engage in casual browsing without looking for something specific.
5   Make a transaction on the website.

Rob's methodology was then adopted by the project, with partner organizations uploading a single-question audience survey to their websites in order to track their audiences' motivations for visiting their websites. These motivations were then tracked against web data captured via Google Analytics, in order to obtain meaningful insights into web behaviours. These insights were drawn from comparisons made across all partner organizations, as well as more deeply for each organization individually.

Insights drawn from comparisons included the following:

• Planning a visit was the most popular category.
• Many organizations' websites are regarded as a professional resource.
• Professional and research-driven audiences generally spend longer on websites.
• Cultural organizations should become better at attracting and supporting casual visitors.

However, a comparative analysis of the data across organizations could tell us only so much. For this exercise to have real value for project participants, a deeper analysis of the data needed to be carried out by each organization and validated against its own organizational engagement strategies, target-audience behaviours and website purpose.

To assist with this, Culture24 generated further data from individual Google Analytics accounts of each organization, connecting the motivational segments to metrics related to content, search and traffic sources. Coupled with the comparative data generated earlier, this represented enough relevant data to enable each organization to begin to undertake a meaningful analysis of behaviours versus motivations for its organization.

For key reflections on this analysis by some of the participant organizations please see pages 25–27 of the Phase 2 report (see 'Further resources' at the end of this chapter).

As a result of this analysis of web behaviours, Culture24 recommended the following for cultural organizations:

• Keep asking yourself 'what are the most important goals for my organization that my website helps people accomplish?'
• Don't just ask what your audience do on your website or how they do it, but also why.
• Learn to love segments in analytic tools.
• Prioritize your design and content decisions based on the patterns of audience behaviour you want to have on your website.
• Keep reviewing your audiences' web behaviours in order to better understand and act on changes.
• Make it a priority to be able to access analytics data from any third-party ticketing websites or systems you may use.

Understanding mobile behaviours

Mobile benchmarking analysis was undertaken across the group to assess if data backed up the perception that audience behaviours were changing dramatically as a result of the increasing use of mobile web devices.

In addition, the need was identified for organizations to analyse closely the detailed web behaviours of their mobile audiences, in order to better serve them, and suggestions were made as to how they might go about doing this.

With increased tablet and multi-device usage meaning that organizations might begin to pour all their efforts into building responsive websites, Seb Chan, Director of Digital and Emerging Media, Cooper-Hewitt Smithsonian National Design Museum, discussed with the group the possible analytics implications of responsive websites.

As a result of this analysis of mobile behaviours, Culture24 recommended the following for cultural organizations:

- If 20% or more of your online audience are visiting your site via mobile devices and you don't have a mobile-friendly site, you need to address this as a priority.
- Track visits from mobile devices, distinguishing between mobile phones and tablets, and keep a close eye on differences and how those differences are changing over time.
- Consider the tools that you may need in order to better understand mobile and tablet users.
- Focus on micro conversions as well as macro conversions when seeking to understand mobile behaviours.

Understanding social media behaviours

Investigations were carried out across the project group to explore existing organizational approaches seeking to engage the social-media behaviours of audiences, as well as examining tools, metrics and methodologies needed to better understand these behaviours.

Organizational analysis was therefore undertaken to review social media strategies, investment expended, platforms used and obstacles faced. A review of existing social media metrics, a qualitative-analysis case study and an updated examination of social media as a referrer to websites were also carried out.

Key reflections from this analysis were then identified, alongside the development of a Social Media Evaluation Framework (see 'Further resources' at the end of this chapter for more information) to help organizations better determine their strategic and practical direction of travel in this area.

As result of this analysis of social media behaviours, Culture24 recommended the following for cultural organizations:

- Use the Culture24 Social Media Evaluation Framework to help you meaningfully interrogate your audience's existing social media behaviours against your organizational goals.
- Consider if driving social media behaviours is the best way to achieve your organizational goals.
- Remember that social media is not free.
- Use interaction and virality rates as a way of evaluating which social media posts users like to engage with.
- Using imagery in your social media posts will drive audience comments and responses.
- Use qualitative analysis to interrogate more deeply the quality and sentiment of conversations taking place on your social media channels.
- If your primary objective for using social media to engage audiences is

to drive them to your website – think again!
- Remember that audience engagement with your organization also occurs outside your own social media channels.

Conducting individual research experiments

As the project ran its course through the various workshops, research tasks and group discussions, four key observations came to inform the final project tasks:

1 Greater insight on digital engagement is achieved when each organization decides what engagement means in the context of its own organizational goals, needs, constraints and knowledge.
2 Organizations need to make better use of available data to help drive these decisions.
3 Organizations would benefit from running their own practical investigations towards this end.
4 Organizations currently lack a framework that could help to guide and structure these investigations.

Taking these observations on board, Culture24 decided that it would be a valuable exercise at the culmination of the project for participant organizations to run their own short individual research experiments. This would allow each organization to utilize the momentum, learning, support and infrastructure built up within the project to date, in order to develop useful insights on aspects of digital audience engagement that were specifically relevant to it.

These individual research experiments would also become exercises in *learning to learn*, identifying the opportunities and challenges in adopting such an approach. They would also ultimately inform the development of a future best practice framework and help Culture24 to support similar future investigations within cultural organizations.

Therefore, between March and June 2013, we asked participating organizations to come up with their own action-research experiment focusing on understanding existing behaviours and/or trying to change these behaviours. Participants were able to report back to the group on these tasks at the final project workshop.

For summaries of some of these research experiments please see the Phase 2 project report (pp. 40–4).

As a result of conducting these individual research experiments, Culture24 recommended the following for cultural organizations:

- If you have a hunch, try to find a way to test it out.
- Incorporate mini online research experiments and testing into your ongoing digital activities.
- Don't try to research everything in one go – small findings can be hugely insightful.
- Validate your results where possible against available benchmarks.
- Don't worry if your experiment fails: this is still a positive outcome.
- Make sure your relationship with your existing technology supplier is fit for purpose to support an experimental approach.
- Realize that undertaking research experiments provides the additional benefit of 'learning to learn'.

Key insights

At the end of the project, Culture24 reflected on the various investigations conducted into audience behaviours, in order to identify key insights for the sector as a whole when thinking about audience engagement.

1 Measure what you value, don't value what you measure

Evidencing, measuring and analysing the ways in which an organization's activities deliver their mission should be an integral part of everyday working life. Understanding what success or failure looks like is the key to knowing if you have achieved either. You could even go so far as to say that failure is only failure if it goes undetected, because any failure detected can be acted on and improved.

For cultural activities, where success criteria (or performance indicators) are often *not* financial, this becomes a search to measure *value*. Within this search for value we can usefully use data analysis to drive better decision making and internal change and, ultimately, to improve impact. Measuring value is subjective and will always be personal.

To better understand digital engagement, cultural organizations need to explore what and whom they value, as well as to understand what their audiences value, before exploring how these values can be enhanced through digital channels.

> We can now be more focused on those metrics that matter to us, and we are able to give reasoning as to why we are measuring what we measure.
>
> Project participant

2 Learn to love segments, analysis and reporting

Without mastering the art of knowing, and then sharing with colleagues what works and what doesn't, how are cultural organizations going to build real digital capacity and understanding?

A well conceived-analytical report that tells the story of how an organization is trying to deliver its mission via its digital activities helps senior management to make decisions based on real data. The ability to segment audience using analytics tools allows organizations to look more deeply into existing behaviours and therefore understand which behaviours represent a positive outcome for them.

> The segmentation analysis work, and the knowledge sharing as a result of this, really forced me to dig in deeper to Google Analytics than I had done before and gave me the knowledge and experience to look meaningfully at the data.
>
> Project participant

3 Focus on demand, not supply

Ensuring a focus on user behaviour and demand and a move away from the institutional, supply-driven model is vital. It means a shift from 'we have these ceramics, how can we tell people about them and improve access to them?' to 'lots of people are interested in pottery, how can we start a conversation about our shared knowledge around our ceramics collection?'

This reframing is an issue that impacts on all aspects of an organization's work – offline and online – and permeates programming, education, fundraising, events, curation, production, retail and research.

> The project's enabled us to think more about types of audience on the website, but also being able to categorize our content to different audiences rather than thinking of content in a departmental structure.
>
> Project participant

4 Understand motivating behaviours

One way for an organization to define engagement is through understanding the changing behaviours of its audiences. Organizations need a way to interpret the metrics they are collecting. Examining them in the context of indicative audience web behaviours allows such interpretation to begin to happen.

Analytics data can tell you what your audience are doing and, in some cases, how they are doing it, but does not give you any clear insight into *why* they are doing it. Nor does analytics offer any certainty that your audience will continue to behave that way in the future. By understanding the motivations of your audience, and exploring this alongside behaviours, a much more complete picture of audience engagement can be drawn.

> Understanding individual motivation, when linked with real behaviour, provides a far more rounded insight into our online audiences.
>
> Project participant

5 Allow time to think, time to change

For cultural organizations attempting any of this, it is vital to be realistic and honest about the time and effort that digital activities take. Organizations need to ensure that they have time to think and space to try things out (and fail), and have the buy-in of leadership.

The speed of change is daunting and difficult to keep up with, even for well-resourced organizations. The birth and death of many online brands and services over recent years is evidence that even those organizations born digital struggle to stay relevant to users. The need to stay relevant also affects how organizations track their relevance and impact. Good evaluation practice is never 'set and forget'. In particular there is a need to be responsive to:

- ongoing changes to measurement tools
- the importance of search and discovery and the benefits of a holistic approach to content
- the value of A/B (see http://en.wikipedia.org/wiki/A/B_testing) and user testing to try stuff out
- the evolution of new platforms and shifting audience loyalties, behaviours and desires.

> Currently the way we report our metrics is fairly ad hoc and doesn't feel like it has a huge impact on what we do. So it was useful to have an incentive to spend time using analytics to ask ourselves questions about what we do and what impact it has.
>
> Project participant

Postscript

Culture24's investigations into how cultural organizations can become better at dealing with issues relating to digital technologies and services, data and measurement have continued into Phase 3 of Let's Get Real, which focuses on the question 'Is your content fit for purpose?'

Thirty-two arts and heritage organizations from across the UK are participating in the project, which kicked off in March 2014 and will culminate in a final report published in early 2015. This question was at the heart of Culture24's 2014 Let's Get Real Conference in Brighton (details of the conference can be found at http://weareculture24.org.uk/lets-get-real-conference).

Chapter conclusion

Cultural heritage institutions are increasingly engaging with their audiences beyond the confines of their own websites and resources. It is therefore essential that institutions are able to measure, track and analyse their impact and engagement across the web. But it is no longer enough simply to capture the classic metrics of page hits and 'Likes' or shares. Instead, the metrics are themselves beginning to evolve, so that we are compelled both to question our motivations and requirements for using web metrics and to ensure that we are capturing and measuring data that answers the questions we feel are most important. Simply because we can capture some kind of data easily doesn't mean that it is the right thing to be measuring and counting.

Web and social media metrics also highlight the increased 'data exhaust' that we all leave behind us as we occupy the web in an increasingly intimate way. While these trails offer institutions greater opportunities for understanding web behaviours and interactions, they also present a number of considerable legal and ethical challenges – challenges that continue to grow in complexity and urgency as the technology outpaces policy and legislation. These legal and ethical challenges will be the topic of our next chapter.

Web and social and media metrics: further resources

If you'd like to find out more about the work described in this chapter, and access further reading and inspiration, below are additional resources for individuals and institutions interested in web and social media metrics for the cultural heritage sector.

More on the case studies
- For broader details of the Let's Get Real action-research initiative, please visit http://weareculture24.org.uk/projects/action-research/.
- For more information on Let's Get Real Phase 2, please visit www.weareculture24.org.uk/projects/action-research/phase-2-digital-engagement.
- For more information on Let's Get Real Phase 3, including the report documenting the project, please visit http://weareculture24.org.uk/projects/action-research/phase-3-fit-for-purpose/.

- For more information about the Social Media Evaluation Framework and how to use it, along with other useful tools and resources, please see the following link: www.weareculture24.org.uk/projects/action-research/phase-2-digital-engagement.

General resources

- Web Metrics Papers from Museums and the Web, www.museumsandtheweb.com/paper_tags/metrics.html.
- Fresh and New(er): discussion of issues around digital media and museums, www.freshandnew.org.
- Strupp, P. An Introduction to Web Metrics, www.libqual.org/documents/admin/arl_emetrics_workshop_june05.pdf.

References

Brewer, J. (2011) The Impact of Impact, *Research Evaluation*, **20** (3), September, 255–6. http://jonathanstray.com/papers/The%20Impact%20of%20Impact.pdf.

Porter, J. (2008) *Designing for the Social Web*, New Riders.

Shirky, C. (2003) 'A group is its own worst enemy', quoted in Benkler, Y. (2006) *The Wealth of Networks: how social production transforms markets and freedom*, Yale University Press, 373.

Stray, J. (2012) Metrics, Metrics Everywhere: how do we measure the impact of journalism? Nieman Lab, 17 August, www.niemanlab.org/2012/08/metrics-metrics-everywhere-how-do-we-measure-the-impact-of-journalism/.

White, D. and Le Cornu, A. (2011) Visitors and Residents: a new typology for online engagement, *First Monday*, **16** (9), http://firstmonday.org/ojs/index.php/fm/article/view/3171/3049.

Case Study 5.1

Achrekar, H., Gandhe, A., Lazarus, R., Ssu-Hsin, Y. and Benyuan, L. (2011) Predicting Flu Trends Using Twitter Data. In *IEEE InfoCon 2011 – IEE Conference on Computer Communications Workshop*, 702–7.

Alexa (2014) How Are Alexa's Traffic Rankings Determined? www.alexa.com/faqs/?p=134.

Association of Leading Visitor Attractions (2014) http://alva.org.uk/details.cfm?p=423.

Behn, R. D. (2003) Why Measure Performance? Different purposes require different measures, *Public Administrative Review*, **63** (5), 586–606.

Compete (2014) Our Data, https://www.compete.com/about-compete/our-data/.

Eysenbach, G. (2011) Can Tweets Predict Citations? Metrics of social impact based on Twitter and traditional metrics of scientific impact, *Journal of Medical Internet Research*, **13** (4), e123, www.jmir.org/2011/4/e123/.

Google (2014) *How Trends Data Is Normalized,*
https://support.google.com/trends/answer/4365533?hl=en&ref_topic=4365599.

Hubbard, D. W. (2011) *Pulse,* John Wiley & Sons.

Quantcast (2014) How Do You Collect Your Data?
https://www.quantcast.com/help?jump=faqs_panelu0026fid=13988.

Stuart, D. (2014) *Web Metrics for Library and Information Professionals,* Facet Publishing.

Thelwall, M. (2009). *Introduction to Webometrics: quantitative web research for the social sciences,* Morgan & Claypool Publishers.

Case Study 5.2

Locke, M. (2013) History of the Internet in 41 behaviours,
www.slideshare.net/SocialTVConference/socialtvconf-presentations-22113-matt-locke-from-storythings.

Stein, R., Fantoni, S. F. and Bowman, G. (2012) *Exploring the Relationship between Visitor Motivation and Engagement in Online Museum Audiences,* Museums and the Web. www.museumsandtheweb.com/mw2012/papers/exploring_the_relationship_between_visitor_mot.

Understanding and managing the risks of analytics

Chapter overview

This chapter brings us close to the end of the book. Yet, we shouldn't confuse its position at the end with any suggestion that it is unimportant or an afterthought. Rather, this is possibly the most important chapter of the book, necessarily following the discussions of how analytics can transform services and collections, and acknowledging that in a relatively new area like analytics, this is less of an ending and more of a beginning.

This chapter provides a single case study exploring the legal and ethical risks that institutions will face in using analytics. The case study offers an overview of the current legal and ethical landscape, providing links to relevant resources and beginning to outline a code of conduct for institutions utilizing data analytics.

• CASE STUDY 6.1 Chowcat, I., Kay, D. and Korn, N., *The legal, risk and ethical aspects of analytics* (p. 157)

Before we explore the case study and its analysis of the legal and ethical risks for institutions exploiting data and analytics, it's worth briefly reflecting on the multi-faceted and nuanced challenges of privacy and data protection, for libraries in particular.

Redrawing the boundaries of privacy

In exploring the implications of the social sharing of content, Eric Hellman (2014) notes the traditional role of the library as a 'haven of privacy', where it is not unheard-of for librarians to go to jail for refusing to provide user records to the authorities (Cowan, 2006 provides a 21st-century example from the US). But, without giving much thought to it, libraries are actively engaging with and encouraging the use of social-media widgets and sharing buttons

(Facebook's 'Like' button probably being the most ubiquitous of all social-sharing widgets). Hellman makes it clear that the use of these widgets and web analytics tools has 'the cumulative effect… that website users can be pretty comprehensively tracked, and if need be, identified, whether they like it or not. In exchange for deploying the trackers, websites get access to the valuable pool of information about their users' (Hellman, 2014). The difficulty for libraries and cultural heritage institutions is that protecting the privacy of users is no longer responding against a clear and well defined threat. Indeed, it may even be perceived as an improved service or better user experience. In adding the kinds of functionality that users might expect – a 'Like' button, for example – libraries may also be undermining some of the values they have traditionally held so dear, such as the user's right to privacy.

As Hellman goes on to make clear, libraries are in a quandary: 'If libraries still think that user privacy is valuable in this age of social media, they need to rethink out their use of web user tracking companies. What disturbs me most is there hasn't been much public discussion about the future role of privacy in library websites, even as it's rapidly being lost.'

Increasingly, the boundaries of privacy are becoming perforated, slowly – almost imperceptibly – changing the shape and feel of what privacy means. Soon, we may find ourselves in a position where we have forgotten what it used to be like, and our perception of privacy will be almost unrecognizable from what it was just a few years ago. There is the potential for the erosion of user privacy to be intimately tied to those pieces of code and algorithms that make the library website work better and make the experience of using the library more enjoyable.

As the boundaries of privacy are redrawn, so there has been an increased focus on the implications for users and a redoubling of effort to shore up the traditional defences against privacy breaches.

Whose data is it anyway?

In response to some of the issues thrown up by the social sharing of content, there are emerging attempts to establish legal frameworks around the ownership and use of data. The European Court of Justice's ruling that there is a 'right to be forgotten' (European Court of Justice, 2014), and the implications of this for Google and others, has begun the encoding into law of the expectation that users should be able to interact with online services and systems on their own terms and, critically, as the owners of any data trails created during those interactions.

But, it is safe to conclude that in such an immature but rapidly developing area the law will be continually outpaced by technological developments.

Despite the increased awareness about the ownership and exploitation of personal data, the genie is, as it were, already out of the bottle. We all expect, and largely assume, that goods and services will be tailored to our specific requirements. Our tolerance for rekeying information, for searching or constantly customizing services, is limited. We allow our data privacy to be compromised for convenience, and are largely complicit in the dissolution of privacy that legal frameworks such as the right to be forgotten aim to try to protect. For example, within an educational environment there is an expectation that the transactional and interaction data created as students move through the institution as part of their educational career will be captured and used for their benefit. While we are rightly concerned by the ethical implications of using this data, we may increasingly be occupied by the question asked by the student who failed or dropped out of their course: 'Why didn't you spot my problems and help me? Why didn't you use my data to prevent me from failing?'

As Chowcat et al. argue in their case study, 'the availability of big data in education carries with it an obligation on institutions for it to be used to benefit both students and the institution… Therefore the complexity of the ethical considerations involved cannot provide an excuse for inaction.' There is, therefore, a data imperative: Data should be used and analysed to benefit and support the user. But this doesn't mean a simple abdication, on the part of the library or institution, of responsibility for user privacy. Rather, that responsibility is more urgent than ever. It may no longer stem from the library or institution's being a 'haven of privacy' but, rather, from its being an educator in privacy, empowering citizens and users to take control and ownership of their own data and privacy and enabling their users to understand and control their personal data flows.

The importance of data flows

We are faced by an interesting paradox: A multitude of tiny incursions into our privacy makes confronting any single breach meaningless, and addressing the whole seemingly impossible. And we are ourselves complicit in the erosion of our privacy, such that notions such as public/private appear as quaint norms from an irrelevant past. Increasingly, we need a new vocabulary to describe the ways in which we might begin wresting back control over our privacy and our ownership of data, and how institutions like libraries might play a role in that renegotiation of personal privacy.

One idea we might begin to explore is that of informational or data flows. We have discussed data flows a lot in this book (if not always explicitly calling them flows) as a way to improve and enhance the institution's ability to capture and analyse interaction data in order to improve services and the user experience. But these data flows are often conceived of as if in a vacuum; the information and data flow independently, without being attached to the users themselves. What if these information and data flows were anchored to the individual, and their use determined by a framework of 'contextual integrity' – the norms and established values associated with the use of data in that particular context?

In her book *Privacy in Context*, Helen Nissenbaum begins to put forward these notions as a language that provides 'a form of expression' for explaining when and why practices that affect the flow of information are troubling and can serve as a basis 'for prescribing courses of action, decisions, policies and designs' (Nissenbaum, 2014). Nissenbaum goes on to say:

> Contextual integrity is defined in terms of informational norms: it is preserved when informational norms are respected and violated when informational norms are breached. The framework of contextual integrity maintains that the indignation, protest, discomfit and resistance to technology-based information systems and practices … invariably can be traced to breaches of context-relative informational norms. Accordingly, contextual integrity is proposed as a benchmark for privacy.
>
> (p. 140)

The notions of privacy that have worked for us till now no longer apply. Notions such as contextual integrity enable us to blur the distinction between private and public, but without breaching the informational norms of a particular situation. Privacy may imply a limitation of access to personal information, whereas a particular context – such as searching a library catalogue – may provide a specific context where access to a personal data flow would be appropriate. But, critically, access to that flow is not at the discretion of others, but is determined by the person whose data it is.

This approach may hardly sound particularly ground breaking, yet it has implications for the way we understand and address privacy dilemmas and personal data in our systems, services and on the web. For example, take the controversy that surrounded Google Street View and the privacy implications of images photographed in real time, where an identifiable man is seen exiting a strip club, female students can be seen sunbathing on Stanford University's campus and car licence plates are clearly visible. A standard reaction was that the images were taken in public places, so they are public. But, Nissenbaum argues, part of being on a public street is that reciprocity is a key part of the informational context: I can see who can see me, and I largely know what's happening around me. If a Google Street View car takes my picture as it goes past, that has broken the tacit agreement. It therefore violates my privacy. The context or social situation is included in any equation.

It may not always be easy to establish what norms prevail for any given context, or there may be nuances to even the most apparently straightforward – like sharing medical data, for example. But this is the point: contextual integrity throws open these complexities and problematic contexts. They are not ignored or treated as simple dichotomies. Indeed, understanding and making explicit these contextual norms for different situations can help to enable a greater sharing of information, rather than restrict it.

Fundamentally, there is an opportunity to begin shifting the discussion away from ridged notions of privacy, and towards notions of data and information flows. Here, data which is anchored to the individual user, and its flow, is determined by the particular context the user finds themselves in. The role of libraries here is particularly interesting. There is both the opportunity for understanding their own contextual norms and values surrounding information flows, and the chance to work with their users to explore their personal data flows and the contextual norms of the different activities and spaces that they may interact with. Librarians may also be well placed to explore with users those contexts where entrenched norms might be challenged or changed, where information flows might be diverted and shared.

As we begin to marry Nissenbaum's notion of contextual integrity and information flow to the examples and principles emerging from current practice and included in the case study below, we begin to move towards a more sophisticated appreciation of how data and analytics can be effectively deployed in libraries and elsewhere. Indeed, we begin to describe a notion of analytics where the user is empowered to make decisions about how data is shared and used and where the library is able to establish a context that makes that use of data an embedded norm of its services.

CASE STUDY 6.1

The legal, risk and ethical aspects of analytics
Ian Chowcat (Sero Consulting), David Kay (Sero Consulting) and Naomi Korn (Naomi Korn Copyright Consultancy)

Context
As universities and colleges increasingly focus on personalized services, even the broad analytics required for library collection development and service improvement needs to take account of specific demographics (e.g. ethnic groups, modes of study) as well as more general 'borrower category' trends. Meanwhile, emergent opportunities to use library data as part of learning analytics imply a more individualized application of trend data ('People like

you …'), moving away from aggregated and highly anonymized treatments.

Consequently, regardless of the approaches offered in library management-dashboard systems (where aggregation typically serves the purposes of collection development), it seems prudent to review legal and ethical considerations relating to library analytics on the same basis as is necessary for the explicitly personalized intentions of learning analytics.

Personalized services, whether relating to library activity or broader learning analytics, involve the collection, storage and analysis of data on user (student, researcher, staff) behaviours and the application of such data to inform decision making and to design interventions (such as resource recommendations and early warnings), which may in turn generate more data. This data can be generated either intentionally, where the student supplies the data in order to meet mutually understood objectives, or unintentionally, in the form of data trails, the incidental by-product of interaction with institutional systems through website clicks, VLE accesses, library borrowing and turnstiles.

However the data is generated, the holding and use of private data on individuals is governed by legal regimes in most if not all developed societies. Here we focus explicitly on the requirements of English law in respect of the key themes of data protection and consent and the related areas of freedom of information, intellectual property rights and licensing and contract law. While the letter of the law will differ in other territories, the same areas will almost certainly be relevant.

In addition, the analysis of data about individuals or generated by them, and the use of such data to intervene in their activities, no matter how benevolent the intention, generates what may be regarded as ethical issues in terms of the norms that should govern the use of data, even when the use of the data is legally compliant.

Legal compliance in itself, while necessary, is insufficient from an ethical standpoint, as it is likely to constrain the permissible use of data within a range of uses but not to dictate how it is used within that range. So, while legal compliance is a necessity for institutions using analytics, the purposes for which analytics are used and a range of issues around the terms on which they are used and the respective roles of the actors involved are an ethical matter, whether they are governed by a contract which specifies mutual obligations beyond legal regulatory requirements over the use of analytics or left to voluntary interactions.

Furthermore, some commentators are concerned that certain approaches should not be treated as if they were unproblematic and unquestionable: for example, how success is defined when analytics are used to promote a goal; and the issue of whether interventions based on analytics are something that the institution and its representatives 'do' to its community of students and researchers or are to be conceived in some other way that involves active participation.

Legal

The legal framework for analytics in the UK is examined in Kay et al. (2012). All data held by an institution is governed by data protection legislation, and the development of analytics raises no new issues of principle, although there may be a need to be clear as to who holds the data for the purposes of registration. New intellectual property rights may arise from the creation of new databases. The increased use and visibility of data may conceivably lead to an increase in the number of freedom of information requests received, and the use and reuse of data, especially if it is shared between institutions, will raise licensing and possibly other contractual issues, depending on who owns the data and how they allow it to be used and by whom. Hence, in developing learning analytics programmes institutions need to be aware of such issues and to ensure that policy and administrative practice are developed appropriately. However, no new issues of principle are raised and for a conscientious institution the legal risk from such work is low.

UK law requires that the consent of the person on whom data is being collected should always be sought; this is normally done when one first signs up to a service on the basis of either an opt-in (you say 'yes' to data being collected) or an opt-out (data is collected unless you explicitly say 'no'). Both approaches have legal standing, although some regard opting out as legally and ethically problematic as a way of securing informed consent (for example, see Clark, 2011 and ESRC, n.d.). Institutions will need a clear policy on this. For consent to be deemed to be proper and informed, clear and transparent information as to what information is collected, and for what range of purposes, needs to be readily available for the user to consult; Kay et al. (2012) cite good commercial examples of statements that achieve this. While informed consent and transparency are a legal requirement, in the UK at least, it should be noted that for many it is also an ethical requirement, to which more than lip-service needs to be paid.

Kay et al. (2012, p. 11) introduce each of these areas of legislation and the associated risk considerations, and include a summary checklist (p. 15). Their paper (p. 9) also maps a range of service scenarios to the legislation, including cases where third parties such as outsourced services are involved.

Overall, then, the legal framework governing the collection and use of analytics requires institutional vigilance and active policy development and implementation through resourcing and processes. It implies that policy in areas such as licensing and contract management may need to be developed, but (except possibly for where the legal requirement for informed consent crosses over with ethical concerns discussed below) no new major issues of principle are raised. Because this is a new domain of activity, then, the application of the law and particular solutions have not generally been subject to legal tests in the courts, and so there is inevitably a degree of risk involved, but it would seem to be low. Given that learning analytics are normally deployed for benevolent reasons, the risk of legal challenge would also seem to be low, although this may depend on how some of the ethical issues discussed below are tackled.

Ethical

The ethical issues surrounding analytics in education are of growing concern and the amount of literature is increasing rapidly.

The issues have even surfaced in the UK national media (Swain, 2013). Compliance with legal frameworks does not determine whether institutions should seek to deploy the explicit and implicit data they collect, nor for what purpose (e.g. Is it to maximize revenue, satisfaction levels or completion rates, or is it to enable each student to achieve their potential? These can point to different and sometimes competing actions.).

Despite theory-laden rhetoric in some papers, there is a great deal of convergence in the literature around ethical rights and obligations in this area, but that does not mean that all the questions are settled. There is a danger of conflating different sorts of analytics-based programmes: the issues raised by student risk-alert systems, for example, are not exactly the same as those for real-time learning-feedback systems or, again, for library-recommender services, although there is some commonality. There is also a danger of ethical absolutism: the discussion tends to be posed in terms of obligations that disregard resource implications that might not feasibly be met.

A full consideration of the ethics of analytics-based programmes would need to be situated in the context of how institutions can best meet their obligations overall in the light of limited resources. Discussing the ethics of analytics in isolation can obscure the need for such all-things-considered judgements that, in practice, authorities have to make. Nevertheless, the ethical issues around analytics need to be articulated, and in particular all actors need to be made aware of the issues that such novel ventures raise.

Ethical issues for institutions

There seems to be a consensus that institutions, and therefore their library functions, should:

- use what they know to promote student success

- use what they know to promote their own well-being – which principally translates into promoting student retention and satisfaction
- support students to successfully manage their own learning
- create and maintain an environment that is conducive to academic success
- ensure that data used in analytics is held in compliance with legal regulations, that it is as accurate and up to date as possible and that anonymization is adequate, with access to individual identifiers appropriately handled.

The main challenge to these assumptions will come from those who argue that the use of data in analytics risks breaching the right to privacy that, arguably, is at the very basis of Western liberal-democratic societies. The use in particular of unintentionally created data robs students of the right to opt-out of data collection; and the pervasiveness of large datasets and presumptions in favour of the primacy of sociability and of sharing undermine a historically hard-won understanding that people flourish best when they have a substantial degree of privacy and solitude. While students have always been obliged to give some data to educational institutions, now the amount of data, the unwitting way in which much of it is generated and its availability for analysis and dissemination pose new challenges of control and privacy that did not arise in traditional systems.

Both Keen (2012) and Brooke (2012) argue that we must learn anew the value of privacy and need to develop new ways of preserving it, perhaps through new commercial services. Educational institutions must therefore assess to what extent it is feasible, let alone desirable, to allow students to opt-out of at least some systems if they wish to. At the same time, they need to do what they can to ensure that students are aware of the implications of behaviour that creates data trails and of the extent to which they can maintain their privacy – consistent with the practicalities of wishing to benefit from the educational opportunities that the institution offers.

Some (e.g. Slade and Prinsloo, 2013) would want to ensure that the notion of 'student success' is not something which institutions define on behalf of students, and also that it should be open to a multi-dimensional understanding: success might be getting the highest possible grade but it might also be seen in terms of gaining understanding, or enriching cultural awareness, or building networks, or in a range of other ways.

Another area of concern is the risk of bias and stereotyping. Analytics based on prior history and trends might lead to judgements (e.g. about student potential or about scope of study) which limited the ability of individuals to out-perform expectations and to develop original or serendipitous approaches to their subjects.

Furthermore, decisions based on analytics can allocate resources on the basis of measures implicit in the analytics (e.g. achieving higher grades) rather than, for example, lead to effort being put into enriching learning for students at all levels or, more broadly, developing the library collection and its use. This can lead to an emphasis on allocating resources according to what can be measured, rather than on the basis of a more qualitative conception of the aims of education.

Some might argue that any remedial skewing of resources to favour one group of students over others goes against the presumption that each student is entitled to equal treatment, and hence equal attention, from the institution. This basic ethical claim for equity gains yet another dimension in an environment where every student is also a fee payer.

However, it is easy to overlook the fact that equality is a complex concept and that it is impossible, in principle and not just in practice, to satisfy everything that it might be seen to require. As a matter of conceptual logic, equality in any one dimension inevitably means inequalities in others. Giving the disadvantaged extra help is to give unequal treatment, albeit with the aim of equalizing outcomes or opportunities. Students who pay equal fees may claim that this entitles each of them to an equal share of resources from the institution; but they may also claim that it entitles each one of them to the share of resources they need in order to achieve an equal outcome. And, to add further complexity, the meaning of 'equal outcome' could be read to mean either literally equal outcomes – which could imply a huge skewing of resources to help the least academically able to perform at the highest levels – or, more realistically, that each is helped to achieve according to their abilities. It is such complexity that has led many moral philosophers to conclude that the ideal which a social system needs to satisfy overall is not equality – since it must always be unequal in some dimensions even if equality is attempted in others – but *fairness*, so that the dimensions in which there is inequality are seen to be morally justified.

Many of these debates about equity and resource allocation are not new. However, the advent of analytics, and the context of a fee paying system, give them added salience when it is the data which drives a considerable proportion of decision making.

Ethical complexity: developing codes of conduct

As can be seen, the ethical issues around learning and library analytics are complex and can appear different according to the perspective from which they are viewed: a business manager may well have different priorities from a faculty member or a librarian, and both may differ from students themselves. These differences need to be handled, and the full implications of analytics-based interventions, and the opportunities they offer as well as their difficulties, need to be teased out.

As many commentators argue, the availability of big data in education carries with it an obligation on institutions to use it to benefit both students and the institution (within the context of an all-things-considered judgement on how scarce resources are to be allocated). Thus the complexity of the ethical considerations involved cannot provide an excuse for inaction. Nor are these ethical considerations very different from those in which the educational enterprise is always involved.

On the other hand, data needs to be used in ways that are consistent with treating students as responsible and active agents who act in awareness of the implications of data and analytics for their educational and life chances.

These considerations therefore imply a further set of ethical responsibilities for institutions wishing to take advantage of analytics to further student success, and academic excellence more broadly. In order to ensure, for both moral and legal reasons, that the issues around data and analytics are presented to staff, faculty and students as clearly and transparently as possible, institutions (and therefore libraries) should

- ensure that measurable dimensions of success – in particular, maximizing grades – do not swamp other considerations
- develop awareness of the limitations of interventions based on analytics and that they point to possibilities and probabilities rather than to certainties
- present analytics-based interventions in a manner that enables users to make their own choices, in particular ensuring that analytics-based interventions do not inhibit enquiry and replace learning with spoon-feeding
- consider how users can be involved in designing analytics-based interventions, e.g. through providing input on what data they find relevant or helpful in achieving their study goals.

As was the case for research ethics in the years following World War 2, codes of conduct for analytics need to be developed that can (a) provide a focus for making explicit many of these issues and (b) provide an opportunity to debate and accommodate the range of perspectives, thereby making productive use of diverse voices (Suthers and Verbert, 2013). There may be different codes for the various actors – institutions, faculty and students. Prinsloo and Slade (2013) analysed policy frameworks governing learning analytics in two institutions (the UK's Open University and UNISA in South Africa) and found that they are limited to institutional concerns. Examples of codes that cover all the actors seem still to be in the very early stages of development (e.g.

https://docs.google.com/file/d/0B4jK4sS8AznvY2NoZWttSXdPTFU/edit). While researchers can propose model codes, these will not fulfil their purpose unless they are elaborated and adopted in an inclusive process by institutions themselves.

Kay et al. (2012, p. 19) compares education-sector considerations with the experience and resulting norms in the research, consumer and social-network domains. Research ethics provides a valuable basis for thinking about the issues raised by analytics, and has the added advantage of recognition within the educational community. The practice adopted by leading business-to-consumer services provides a clear and legally grounded approach that is likely to be readily understood by the public in much of the world. Kay et al.'s paper recognizes the challenge to the education community as to whether it should review its ethical position on account of changing attitudes and expectations in the digital realm with which learners and researchers are increasingly associated. It concludes that, at the very least, even if ethical norms are not immutable or self-evident, practice in other sectors suggests useful candidate approaches.

Conclusion: compelling considerations and guiding principles

There are now compelling motivations driving the development of analytics capabilities in the education sector:

- Responses to economic and competitive pressures may be derived from business intelligence.
- Analytics practice is strongly linked to modern enterprise management.
- Users, especially born-digital generations, appear increasingly to expect personalized services that are responsive to profile, need and interest – and are therefore more likely to be content for their data to be used to those ends.

In considering the collection and processing of such data, institutions need to balance risks and rewards with legal and policy obligations as well as with the expectations of their community by

- aligning use of personal-activity data and business intelligence with their overall mission and motives
- weighing the benefits and costs of putting in place policies, procedures and tools for organizational legal and risk compliance
- adapting governance frameworks and developing staff awareness to cover the responsibilities related to such data
- taking account of capture and exploitation of student – or researcher – activity data by individual academics and service providers (both

within and external to the institution) including shared services.

However, the exercise of due diligence is hampered by the speed of developments in the online world and the pressure on institutions not to be left behind in the competition for students and for research funding. The education sector faces two issues:

- *the level of legal 'maturity'*: there is a lack of precedent to indicate the application of the law in the digital environment and therefore uncertainty remains about legal interpretation
- *comparable ethical settings*: bearing in mind, therefore, that practice and precedent in education are relatively underdeveloped, useful exemplars might be found in research and medical ethics and in retail and online consumer services; however, there remains an underlying question as to whether education is in some respects special.

As Voltaire's Candide might have reflected, we are faced with the imperative to seek out the 'best of all possible worlds':

- In assuring educational benefits, not least supporting student progression, maximizing employment prospects and enabling personalized learning, it is incumbent on institutions to adopt key principles from research ethics.
- As businesses, post-compulsory educational institutions are facing the same business drivers and globalized competitive pressures as face any organization in the consumer world.
- To satisfy the expectations of the 'born digital'/'born social' generations, there is likely to be a need to take on ethical considerations which may run contrary to the sensibilities of previous generations, especially in respect of the trade-off between privacy and service.

Notwithstanding these tensions, we conclude that there are common principles that can provide for good practice:

- *clarity*: open definition of purpose, scope and boundaries, even if that is broad and in some respects open-ended
- *comfort and care*: consideration for both the interests and the feelings of the data subject, and vigilance with regard to exceptional cases
- *choice and consent*: informed individual opportunity to opt-out or opt-in
- *consequence and complaint*: recognition that there may be unforeseen consequences, and therefore provision of mechanisms for redress.

Chapter conclusion

As we come to the end, we find that we are actually at the beginning; at the beginning of understanding and responding to the complex legal and ethical implications of analytics for our privacy and, indeed, the implications for our social lives more generally. As our case study demonstrates, in many ways the legal aspects of analytics are the least challenging. We simply have to respond and conform to the legal requirements that are laid out for us. The problem we face with the legal frameworks that we have is that the technological developments are happening so rapidly that the legal side of things inevitably lags behind. We therefore face the ethical consequences of analytics without frameworks or legal precedent; we must begin constructing our own ethical approaches to how we collect, analyse and act upon our users' data. Our final case study has begun to provide us with a number of strategies for addressing this need for an ethical framework for how we exploit analytics in libraries and the cultural heritage sector in general.

Understanding the risks of analytics: further resources

If you'd like to find out more about the work described in this chapter, and access further reading and inspiration, below are additional resources for individuals and institutions interested in the legal and ethical risks and challenges for libraries and cultural heritage organizations more generally.

Additional resources

- Cetis analytics series (a number of case studies on the ethics of analytics), http://publications.cetis.ac.uk/c/analytics.
- Educause Library Analytics Toolkit, www.educause.edu/library/analytics.
- Ethics, Big Data, and Analytics: a model for application, www.educause.edu/ero/article/ethics-big-data-and-analytics-model-application.
- Library Analytics and Metrics Project (LAMP) Principles, http://jisclamp.mimas.ac.uk/category/legal-and-ethical.

References

Cowan, A. L. (2006) Four Librarians Finally Break Silence in Records Case, *New York Times*, www.nytimes.com/2006/05/31/nyregion/31library.html?_r=1&.
European Court of Justice (2014) Fact Sheet on the Right To Be Forgotten, C-131/12. http://ec.europa.eu/justice/data-protection/files/factsheets/factsheet_data_protection_en.pdf.

Hellman, E. (2014) Libraries Are Giving Away the User-privacy Store, http://go-to-hellman.blogspot.co.uk/2014/08/libraries-are-giving-away-user-privacy.html.

Nissenbaum, H. (2014) *Privacy in Context: technology, policy and the integrity of social life*, Stanford University Press.

Case Study 6.1

Brooke, H. (2012) *The Revolution Will Be Digitised*, Windmill Books.

Clark, P. (2011) Can I Opt Out of Opting In? Location data and the consent conundrum,
www.taylorwessing.com/download/article_optout.html#.U5hqmxba629.

ESRC (n.d.) Research Ethics Guidebook: consent,
www.ethicsguidebook.ac.uk/Opt-in-and-opt-out-sampling-94.

Kay, D. et al. (2012) *Legal, Risk and Ethical Aspects of Analytics in Higher Education*, Jisc CETIS Analytics Series No. 6, http://publications.cetis.ac.uk/2012/500.

Keen, A. (2012) *Digital Vertigo*, Constable.

Prinsloo, P. and Slade, S. (2013) An Evaluation of Policy Frameworks for Addressing Ethical Considerations in Learning Analytics. In *Third Conference on Learning Analytics and Knowledge* (LAK 2013), 8–12 April, Leuven, Belgium.

Slade, S. and Prinsloo, P. (2013) Learning Analytics: ethical issues and dilemmas, *American Behavioral Scientist* (online first),
http://oro.open.ac.uk/36594/2/ECE12B6B.pdf.

Suthers, D. D. and Verbert, K. (2013) Learning Analytics as a "Middle Space". In *Proceedings of the Third International Conference on Learning Analytics and Knowledge*, New York, 1–4.

Swain, H. (2013) 'Are Universities Collecting Too Much Information on Staff and Students? *Guardian*, 5 August, www.theguardian.com/education/2013/aug/05/electronic-data-trail-huddersfield-loughborough-university.

Conclusion: towards a data-driven future?

Data is increasingly digital air: the oxygen we breathe and the carbon dioxide that we exhale. It can be a source of both sustenance and pollution.

(Boyd and Crawford, 2011)

There is no escaping it, our future will increasingly be data driven. Data will be the fuel that powers our services and systems. We'll need to be comfortable dealing with the advantages as well as the by-products and unforeseen consequences. We have a chance to begin shaping this future before we find ourselves moulded by it.

There is a sense that we are at a frontier. Our 'wild west' is before us, and we are at the start of a push forward. Being analytics pioneers means carving new paths, developing our own tactics and strategies and confronting the challenges present in the landscape, such as the ethical dilemmas with which analytics confronts us. As the chapters and case studies in this book have tried to demonstrate, there are a growing number of experiments and examples that we can begin to learn from and build on, so as to construct our own practices, strategies and frameworks.

As we begin to further explore and settle this new terrain, there are a number of lessons we can take from our case studies to help prepare us for the journey.

We need to put the needs of our users before those of the department. As libraries and cultural heritage institutions we need to re-orientate our precious and limited resources from the back-office, administrative processes and systems to the user- or visitor-facing services. For many of the authors of the case studies in this book, their work on analytics and user data remains a relatively small part of their roles. This must change, in order to ensure that libraries and institutions are able to deliver the kinds of services and experiences which their users expect.

The roles we have in libraries and cultural heritage institutions will evolve. Chapter 4 described the work of researchers and ethnographers working within or closely with libraries to help inform physical and online service development. A number of the case studies describe roles or skill-sets that would be more common in a technology company: user-experience developers, data analysts, information architects, anthropologists and so on. The roles we associate with libraries are changing, and will continue to evolve and change to reflect the increasing role of data and analytics in the digital information environment.

For librarians, archivists and curators in general there will be a need to develop more familiarity with data analysis and to improve general data literacy within the professions. This will also be driven by the convergence of other developments, such as research data on the changing role of libraries, making it a compelling requirement for library staff in the future.

Of course, the technology will not remain static, but threatens to develop at ever more rapid speeds. New technologies, such as the Internet of Things, where 'things' begin to talk to each other (your car with your garage, your fridge with your supermarket), imply that data will only grow in importance and centrality. Associated with this are the legal and ethical considerations that these new developments will entail. Libraries can, and should, have a critical role to play here, helping their users to navigate this increasingly complex and data-driven digital environment. Indeed, while the technological landscape will get ever more complex, it is analytics itself that can provide us with a safe harbour in this digital maelstrom.

In a world transfigured by the fluidity and constancy of change, analytics provides us with something concrete to hold on to, and can be an anchor in a rapidly evolving technological, social and economic ocean. It anchors us to our users and audiences, enabling us to get a picture of what they are doing and how and why they are performing certain activities. It ensures that our resources and effort are directed where they will have the greatest impact and value. Not only are libraries ideally placed to take advantage of analytics for the benefit of their users, but analytics have the potential to provide libraries with a new future.

At this new frontier we can begin to invent new and more human ways for people to interact with information.

Reference

Boyd, D. and Crawford, K. (2011) Six Provocations for Big Data, *A Decade in Internet Time: Symposium on the Dynamics of the Internet and Society.*

Index

academic engagement, University of Minnesota 58–66
actionable analysis, analytic experiments 49
Activity Data programme, Jisc 7, 15
aim, this book's xxv
Altmetrics 117
analytic experiments, library impact and value 49–50
analytics, defining xxx
analytics guiding principles 164–6
analytics potential, libraries 14–16
analytics toolkit, Harvard Library 28–35
Association of American College and Universities 64

basis for data analysis 4
bias, ethical aspect of analytics 161–2
big data 2–5
   analytics potential 14–16
   defining 2
   dual approach, small/big data 3–5
   key factors 14
   shared analytics service for academic libraries 14–21
blogs, cultural heritage institutions (CHIs) 126–7
British Library 3
   Document Supply Service 27
   global traffic services 123–4
   search engine optimization (SEO) 129–31
   semantic web 135
   social media metrics 131–4
   social media views 125–6
   user behaviour 121–6
   web impact 117–36

   web impact assessment 128–9
British Museum
   global traffic services 123–4
   Google Trends 124
   search engine optimization (SEO) 129–31
   semantic web 135
   social media metrics 131–4
   social media views 125–6
   user behaviour 121–6
   web impact 117–36
   web impact assessment 128–9

CCM *see* Copac Collections Management tool
chapter summaries xxviii–xxix
CHIs *see* cultural heritage institutions
codes of conduct, ethical aspect of analytics 162–4
collaborative spaces for students
   University of North Carolina, Charlotte 98–107
collection profiling
   Copac Collections Management (CCM) tool 39–40
   University of St Andrews 40
collections turn, data-driven collections management 24
combining data, University of York 40–1
consent, legal aspect of analytics 159
Copac Collections Management (CCM) tool 15, 23, 35–43
   collection profiling 39–40
   future activities 41–3
   pilot 36–7
   stock management 38–9
   University of Manchester 39

University of Sheffield 38
University of York 40–1
cost savings, dual approach, small/big
    data 4
Counting Online Usage of Networked
    Electronic Resources (COUNTER)
    standards, Harvard Library 30
course based recommendations, RISE
    (Recommendations Improve the
    Search Experience) 10
crowdsourcing applications, cultural
    heritage institutions (CHIs) 127–8
cultural heritage institutions (CHIs)
    blogs 126–7
    crowdsourcing applications 127–8
    digital engagement 136–50
    expectations 138
    global traffic services 123–4
    Google Trends 124
    pressures 138
    recommendations for 144–6
    search engine optimization (SEO)
        129–31
    semantic web 135
    social media metrics 131–4
    social media views 125–6
    URIs (Uniform Resource Identifiers)
        129–31
    user behaviour 121–6
    user traces 126–35
    web impact 117–36
    web impact assessment 128–9
Culture24, digital engagement 136–50

data collection
    diaries 86, 95–6
    OCLC Research 82–4
    online survey 87
    semi-structured interviews 85–6, 93–5
    University of Minnesota 58–9
    Visitors and Residents (V&R) project
        84–7, 93–6
data-driven collections management 23–
    45
    collections turn 24
    Copac Collections Management (CCM)
        tool 35–43
    Harvard Library, analytics toolkit 28–
        35
    local collections management 24–6
    national collection management 27–8
    resources, additional 44–5
data-driven future 169–70
    Library Analytics and Metrics Project
        (LAMP) 20
data flows 155–7

data literacy, dual approach, small/big
    data 4
data ownership 154–5
Data Protection Act (1998) 7–8
Dataviews Dashboard (By the Numbers)
    Harvard Library 31, 32, 33
    North Carolina State University
        Library 30
definitions xxix–xxx
    analytics xxx
    big data 2
    metrics xxx
    small data 2
demand focus, digital engagement 148
demographics
    Library Impact Data Project (LIDP)
        54–5
    University of Minnesota 61–2
diaries, data collection 86, 95–6
digital engagement 136–50
    cultural heritage institutions (CHIs)
        136–50
    defining 141
    demand focus 148
    key insights 147–9
    macro perspective 141
    micro perspective 141–3
    mobile behaviours, understanding
        144–5
    motivating behaviours 148–9
    recommendations for CHIs 144–6
    research experiments 146–7
    segmentation analysis 148
    shared issues 141–3
    social media behaviours,
        understanding 145–6
    time for thinking and changing 149
    value, measuring 147–8
    web behaviours, understanding 143–4
diversity of data, analytic experiments 49
Document Supply Service, British Library
    27
dual approach, small/big data 3–5

EBSCO Discovery API, RISE
    (Recommendations Improve the
    Search Experience) 9
enquiry based recommendations, RISE
    (Recommendations Improve the
    Search Experience) 10
equality, ethical aspect of analytics 162
ethical aspects of analytics 153–66
    bias 161–2
    codes of conduct 162–4
    equality 162
    ethical complexity 162–4

ethical responsibilities 163–4
institutions 160–2
stereotyping 161–2
student success 161
ethics, library impact and value 50
ethnographic techniques 96–108
ExLibris, informing personalized
recommendations 6
expansion based recommendations, RISE
(Recommendations Improve the
Search Experience) 10

focus on data, dual approach, small/big
data 4
future
Copac Collections Management (CCM)
tool 41–3
data-driven future 20, 169–70
web metrics and analytics 116–17

gamifying collections, local collections
management 26
global traffic services, cultural heritage
institutions (CHIs) 123–4
Google Trends 124

Harvard Library
analytics toolkit 28–35
Checkout the Checkouts 29, 31
Counting Online Usage of Networked
Electronic Resources (COUNTER)
standards 30
Dataviews Dashboard (By the
Numbers) 31, 32, 33
Library of Congress (LOC)
classification data 33
Library of Congress Subject Heading
(LCSH) hierarchy 31–4

impact, library see library impact and
value
impact, web see web impact
Institutional Repository Usage Statistics
(IRUS) 15
Internet of Things 170
IRUS see Institutional Repository Usage
Statistics

Jisc
Activity Data programme 7, 15
MOSAIC (Making our Scholarly
Activity Information Count) project
6

shared analytics service for academic
libraries 14–21
Journal Impact Factor 117
Journal Usage Statistics Portal (JUSP) 15

LAMP see Library Analytics and Metrics
Project
LCSH see Library of Congress Subject
Heading hierarchy
learning analytics xxvii–xxviii
legal aspects of analytics 153–66
library analytics, diversity xxv–xxvi
Library Analytics and Metrics Project
(LAMP)
analysis 18–19
community 19–20
data 16–18
data-driven future 20
shared analytics service for academic
libraries 16–21
library collaborative spaces for students
98–107
library effectiveness, measuring 82–96
Library Game 26
library impact and value 47–75
analytic experiments 49–50
ethics 50
resources, additional 75
student success 47–8
University of Huddersfield 15, 51–8
University of Minnesota 58–66
Library Impact Data Project (LIDP) 15,
51–8
analysing the data 52–3
demographics 54–5
discipline 55–6
further research 56–7
original project 53–4
retention 56
strategic drivers 57
Library of Congress (LOC) classification
data 33
Library of Congress Subject Heading
(LCSH) hierarchy 31–4
library roles, evolving 169–70
library usage/access points, University of
Minnesota 59–61
LIDP see Library Impact Data Project
LOC see Library of Congress classification
data
local collections management 24–6
gamifying collections 26
Library Game 26
patron-driven acquisition (PDA) 25
SCVNGR 26

MACON project (Mobilising Academic
    Content Online) 13
Maine Shared Collections Strategy (MSCS)
    27
Manchester Information and Associated
    Services (Mimas) 15
Marketing Cube, University of
    Wollongong 73–4
metrics, defining xxx
Metridoc 3
Mimas see Manchester Information and
    Associated Services
mobile behaviours, understanding 144–5
MOSAIC (Making our Scholarly Activity
    Information Count) project,
    informing personalized
    recommendations 6
motivating behaviours, digital
    engagement 148–9
MSCS see Maine Shared Collections
    Strategy

National Archives
    global traffic services 123–4
    search engine optimization (SEO) 129–
        31
    social media metrics 131–4
    social media views 125–6
    user behaviour 121–6
    web impact 117–36
    web impact assessment 128–9
national collection management
    Document Supply Service 27
    Maine Shared Collections Strategy
        (MSCS) 27
    National Monograph Strategy (NMS)
        28
    UK Research Reserve (UKRR) 27
National Gallery
    global traffic services 123–4
    search engine optimization (SEO) 129–
        31
    social media metrics 131–4
    social media views 125–6
    user behaviour 121–6
    web impact 117–36
    web impact assessment 128–9
National Monograph Strategy (NMS) 28
National Student Survey (NSS) 48
Natural History Museum
    global traffic services 123–4
    search engine optimization (SEO) 129–
        31
    social media metrics 131–4
    social media views 125–6
    user behaviour 121–6

web impact 117–36
web impact assessment 128–9
NMS see National Monograph Strategy
North Carolina State University Library,
    Dataviews Dashboard (By the
    Numbers) 30
NSS see National Student Survey

OCLC Research
    data collection 82–4
    library effectiveness, measuring 82–96
    qualitative research 82–96
online survey, data collection 87
Open Knowledge Foundation 2
Open University (OU) Library Services
    informing personalized
        recommendations 5–13
    MACON project (Mobilising Academic
        Content Online) 13
    RISE (Recommendations Improve the
        Search Experience) 7–13

patron-driven acquisition (PDA), local
    collections management 25
privacy 153–7, 158, 161
Project Information Literacy, University of
    Minnesota 63–4

qualitative research 79–109
    collaborative spaces for students 98–
        107
    evaluation of library services 82–4
    library effectiveness, measuring 82–96
    methods 81–96
    OCLC Research 82–96
    resources, additional 108–9
    skills 81–2
    user experience 79–81
    user needs 81
    Visitors and Residents (V&R) project
        84–96

Research Libraries UK (RLUK) 16
retention, University of Minnesota 58–66
RISE (Recommendations Improve the
    Search Experience)
    approach 7
    background 5–7
    data 7–9
    interface 9
    Open University (OU) Library Services
        7–13
    recommendation types 10–11
    users' perspective 11–12
risk aspects of analytics 153–66

RLUK *see* Research Libraries UK
roles, evolving 169–70

SCONUL *see* Society of College, National
        and University Libraries
SCVNGR 26
search engine optimization (SEO), cultural
        heritage institutions (CHIs) 129–31
searching, streetlight effect xxvi–xxvii
segmentation analysis, digital engagement
        148
semantic web, cultural heritage
        institutions (CHIs) 135
semi-structured interviews, data collection
        85–6, 93–5
SEO *see* search engine optimization
service development, analytic experiments
        49
shared analytics service for academic
        libraries 14–21
    Library Analytics and Metrics Project
        (LAMP) 16–21
small data 2–5
    defining 2
    dual approach, small/big data 3–5
social media behaviours, understanding
        145–6
social media metrics
    cultural heritage institutions (CHIs)
        131–4
    resources, additional 150–1
social media views, cultural heritage
        institutions (CHIs) 125–6
social web 114–16
Society of College, National and
        University Libraries (SCONUL) 16
space assessment, library 104–7
stereotyping, ethical aspect of analytics
        161–2
stock management
    Copac Collections Management (CCM)
        tool 38–9
    University of Manchester 39
    University of Sheffield 38
streetlight effect xxvi–xxvii
student success
    ethical aspect of analytics 161
    library impact and value 47–8
    University of Minnesota 58–66
    University of Wollongong 66–74

time for thinking and changing, digital
        engagement 149

UK Research Reserve (UKRR) 27

University College London 3
University of Huddersfield, Library
        Impact Data Project (LIDP) 15, 51–8
University of Manchester
    Copac Collections Management (CCM)
        tool 39
    Manchester Information and
        Associated Services (Mimas) 15
    stock management 39
University of Minnesota 58–66
    academic engagement 58–66
    circulation, library usage/access point
        60
    data collection 58–9
    demographics 61–2
    digital access, library usage/access
        point 59–60
    impact of the study 63–5
    instruction, library usage/access point
        60
    library impact and value 58–66
    library usage/access points 59–61
    Project Information Literacy 63–4
    reference, library usage/access point 61
    retention 58–66
    student success 58–66
    workstation usage, library usage/access
        point 60
University of North Carolina, Charlotte
        96–108
    collaborative spaces for students 98–
        107
    ethnographic techniques 96–108
    space assessment 104–7
University of Pennsylvania 3
University of Sheffield
    Copac Collections Management (CCM)
        tool 38
    stock management 38
University of St Andrews, collection
        profiling 40
University of Wollongong 66–74
    impact of library use 66–74
    Library Cube 66–74
    Marketing Cube 73–4
    student success 66–74
University of York
    combining data 40–1
    Copac Collections Management (CCM)
        tool 40–1
URIs (Uniform Resource Identifiers),
        cultural heritage institutions (CHIs)
        129–31
US Library of Congress 3
user behaviour, cultural heritage
        institutions (CHIs) 121–6

user traces, cultural heritage institutions (CHIs) 126–35

V&R project *see* Visitors and Residents project
value, library *see* library impact and value
value, measuring 147–8
Visitors and Residents (V&R) project 84–96
    data collection 84–7, 93–6
    diaries 95–6
    findings 87–91
    implications for library services and systems 91–3
    methods 93–6
    research design 84–7
    semi-structured interviews 93–5

web behaviours, understanding 143–4

web impact
    Altmetrics 117
    British Library 117–36
    British Museum 117–36
    cultural heritage institutions (CHIs) 117–36
    Journal Impact Factor 117
    National Archives 117–36
    National Gallery 117–36
    Natural History Museum 117–36
    reasons for measuring 118–20
    tools 120, 121
web impact assessment, cultural heritage institutions (CHIs) 128–9
web metrics and analytics
    cultural heritage sector 114
    future 116–17
    importance 116